TAMING
THE TEMPER

HOW TO MANAGE THE RAGING FIRE WITHIN US
AND PRESERVE OUR RELATIONSHIPS

A PERSONAL OR GROUP STUDY

WITH WORKBOOK
QUESTIONS AND ANSWERS

DONALD E. JONES, PHD

J & A Book Publishers
www.jabookpublishers.com

ISBN-13:978-1946368263
ISBN-10:1946368261

CONTENTS

(Each chapter contains workbook questions at the end.)

Introduction

Being Patient with Peter: The Lord's Example

In Matthew 14, we are provided with a perfect example of the patience of our Lord with Peter and his impulsive ways. After the feeding of the 5,000, Jesus sent His disciples by boat across the Jordan giving Himself time to disperse the crowd and find a place to pray. About the fourth watch of the night (3:00am - 6:00am), the boat was being battered by waves from powerful winds, and Jesus was seen by His disciples walking on the water. At first, they thought it was some kind of an apparition and screamed in fear, "It's a ghost!" Then Jesus cried out for them not to be afraid and identified Himself. In verse 28-29, the apostle Matthew describes Peter's bold response, "Peter answered him and said, 'Lord, if it is you, command me to come to you on the waters.' He said, Come!'"

So, Peter got out of the boat, walked on the water, and headed toward Jesus. Then he looked up and saw the great wind all around him. His eyes turned toward the sea, and he saw the powerful waves. Even in the presence of the Son of God, He became frightened and began to sink. He cried out for Jesus to save him. The Lord responded by immediately stretching out His hand and taking hold of him. Then He looked at the disciple and asked, "You of little faith why do you doubt?" Then, Jesus walked Peter on the water to the safety of the boat, and everything was calm.

There are many other reactions Jesus could have chosen as Peter began sinking; the most obvious would be anger. If the Lord had a bad temper as many of us do, He might have

1

said, "Here we go again, man of such little faith. This time sink then maybe you'll come to realize who I am!" He could have said, "Peter what is wrong with you? Are you stupid? You were just walking on the water! Get your faith together and rise from the sea because I am not going to help you again!" Jesus could have declared, "You're out! You are no longer one of My disciples. I have had just about enough of your nonsense. Save yourself!" Instead, Jesus was patient.

All of these angry responses to Peter's lack of faith would have been wrong, led to Peter's injury or even death, and destroyed their relationship. Yet, these are the kinds of temper tantrums we will often engage in with those we love. Sometimes, we are the ones who must tolerate the angry outbursts of others. We are in relationships with people just like Jesus was with Peter. Our spouses, partners, children, friends, neighbors, fellow students, co-workers, social media community, team players, church members, acquaintances, and even the strangers we meet have many flaws, numerous weaknesses, and make lots of mistakes. They even sin just like Peter and just like us. They may have different values, points of view, and ways of doing things that we may not like or understand just like Peter and us.

Jesus never let His feelings get control of Him but always responded in a patient manner. Though, Jesus was perfect, the Bible indicates that He was tempted in all things as we are. In Hebrews 4:15, the author asserts this very thing, "For we don't have a high priest who can't be touched with the feeling of our infirmities, but one who has been in all points tempted like we are, yet without sin." Yes, the Lord Jesus was probably tempted to leave Peter where he was but did not. Since we are to emulate our Savior and Lord, we must also find the patience we need to build relationships rather than to destroy them. In 1 John 2:6, the apostle declares that we should walk and live as Jesus did. This includes patience.

In our relationship with Jesus, we love the Lord and yet make mistakes, misunderstand His words and actions, and even fail to trust Him. We let the winds and torrents of our lusts and desires get in the way of our devotion to Him. We allow the stormy seas of trouble and tribulation to make us doubt His intentions and power. We allow the flowing waters and winds of our busy lives to make us treat Jesus as an apparition and not a real person. Yet, regardless of how far we have sunk in our foolishness, stupidity, weaknesses, and even rebellious sin, He always reaches His hand out to restore the relationship we have with Him. Does He not?

The Lord Jesus is always willing to accept our numerous struggles, tolerate our weaknesses, and forgive our sin. He is constantly reaching out to make peace with us. At every turn, Jesus, our Father God, and His Father, and the Spirit are ready to reconcile and restore the conflicts we bring into our relationship with Him. And we must do the same with others. We should remember that we are two imperfect Peter's in our relationships; we are not one perfect person together with one imperfect person. Our imperfections and differences will lead to conflict and in the midst of this our anger cannot be unleashed. It will only bring additional conflict and never peace. In Romans 12:18, Paul entreats us, "If it is possible, as much as it is up to you, be at peace with all men." God wants the conflicts between us and others (whether believers or unbelievers) to be resolved, and anger does not allow for this to occur.

In Matthew 5, Jesus discusses the various heart attitudes people in His kingdom should not possess. After speaking of anger, the Lord presents a general principle of living in His kingdom on Earth. In verses 23-24, He explains, "If therefore you are offering your gift at the altar, and there remember that your brother has anything against you, leave your gift there before the altar, and go your way. First be reconciled to your brother, and then come and offer your gift." The Lord wants reconciliation.

Unfortunately, our anger and temper can get in the way. Not only can it cause a conflict, but it can hinder the conflict from being resolved, add more conflict, and even completely destroy the relationship instead. Though I am using the term "taming the temper," the bible actually calls it "putting away anger." This is the expression the apostle Paul uses in his discussion of what Christians are to do with their anger.

When there is conflict, rather than allow the anger inside us to rage, we should tame our tempers and hold out our hands to resolve the conflict and reconcile the relationship. This book will provide a biblical and supernatural way to tame the temper and demonstrate the patience of the Lord.

Chapter 1

Understanding the Inferno: A Typical Scenario

When we unleash our anger and allow our tempers to rage out of control, they can become fiery infernos that burn down all relationship in their paths. Perhaps, you have been involved in this typical scenario of the fiery inferno. Have you ever had or heard a conversation with a spouse, parent, or friend that went something like this? You might say, "Oh, I am so upset! It's almost family reunion time, and this year I wanted to stay at the big family cabin at the lake. For the last three years, everyone else in the family got to pick where we went, and it is my turn now.

Then my younger brother called me and described the horrible time he had last summer at the family cabin with his asthma. Apparently, the altitude is too high and the air too thin for him. He spent the entire week trying to catch his breath. Now he wants to have the reunion near a beach, where he can breathe freely. That is not what I want! So, we got into this big argument. Oh, I am so angry! What a wimp! I'm telling you it is all in his head. This time, I will not bend. I want what I want for a change. He better watch out, when I get angry, there is no telling what I might do."

The person in this scenario let his anger takeover and his relationships with his brother and others in the family may be completely destroyed. This raging like a fire out of control has happened to all of us, but it is not God's way. It has never been God's way. Many of the conflicts we experience in our relationships are due to or are intensified by anger. We get angry and want to fight it out with our words and even our fists. This only leads to more anger.

In a conflict, the biggest hindrance will be our anger. This beast can rear its ugly head during any step in the conflict resolution process. It can and will destroy all the progress we might have made in a matter of minutes using just a few words. Anger is able to build a wall so high that any words or actions to restore the relationship can't be heard or seen. It can spread like fire to anyone connected to the relationship. Their families, friends, church members, co-workers, and fellow students may be forced to take sides and divisions can occur that may never be restored. The ones who remain neutral may be ostracized by either or both parties. Like a snake, a temper can spit its wicked venom poisoning every relationship in its path.

This displeases God the Father. In 1 Corinthians 1:10, Paul entreats the Corinthians to be unified and resolve their disputes, "Now I beg you, brothers, through the name of our Lord, Jesus Christ, that you all speak the same thing and that there be no divisions among you, but that you be perfected together in the same mind and in the same judgment." Later in chapter 12, verse 25, he explains, "That there should be no division in the body, but that the members should have the same care for one another." This is critical biblical principle for believers to follow in their relationships.

We are told throughout the Scriptures that the Lord God wants peace and unity. In 1 Thessalonians 5:13, Paul writes, "Be at peace among yourselves." Then in Hebrews 12:14, it says, "Follow after peace with all men." Anger destroys this peace and unity in our relationships. As a result, this crazed beast of negative emotions and feelings must be prevented, if possible, managed if experienced, and all of its expressions in thoughts, words, and deeds must be eliminated. It should never be allowed to reign free and run amuck. This incensed monster will shatter all relationships including church unity, marriage unions, parent-child bonds, and friendships. I use disturbing images due to the disturbing destruction that can occur when a temper is not tamed.

Often times, anger will actually add to the conflicts we are trying to resolve. In Psalm 37:8, the wise King David warns that unleashing our temper "leads only to evildoing." If we are able to control our anger, we may even prevent the conflict from occurring in the first place or at least be able to resolve it quickly and efficiently. When angry feelings are prevented, managed, or responded to appropriately, then relationships will remain strong and save us a huge amount of trouble and difficulties we create for ourselves. If we are also able to prevent the expression of another's anger or respond to it appropriately, another mess will not be created for us to resolve. We must never unleash this fiery inferno upon others.

Study Questions

Directions: Now that you have read this chapter, answer the following questions. Answers to the questions regarding the text can be found in chapter nine.

1. According to the author, the typical scenario concerned what event?

2. According to the author, what was the conflict about?

3. When the author compares the expression of our anger in relationships with the building of a wall, the spreading of a fire, and the spitting of venom, what does he mean?

4. According to 1 Corinthians 1:10-12 and 12:25, what should never be found in Christian relationships?

5. According to 1 Thessalonians 5:13 and Hebrews 12:14, what are we to seek in our relationships?

6. According to Psalm 37:8, what might the unleashing of our temper actually add to a relationship?

7. Have you had a similar experience to the typical scenario?

Chapter 2

Extinguishing the Blaze:
A Scriptural Principle

The biblical principle that governs our anger involves the full extinguishing of the blaze started by the unleashing of tempers. Let's begin with a discussion of the Lord's cleansing of the temple. Whenever anger is discussed, this is always brought up. Many believers think because Jesus expressed His anger, the saints may express theirs. They usually cite the Lord's cleansing of the temple as proof that there is a "righteous" anger that can be expressed.

Since Jesus expressed His anger and we are to be just like Him, we may do the same. The only caveat is that it must be righteous. We can only get angry at things which make God angry. Sometimes, we might have to overturn some tables in the lives of people. Though this may sound very logical, even compelling, Jesus did not cleanse the temple in anger.

Jesus cleansed the temple on two different occasions from the same motivation: greedy people were taking advantage of the poor by charging exorbitant prices for the foods and animals they needed for their sacrifices. To stop this wicked practice, Jesus overturned their tables and threw them out. Due to their hardened, cold hearts, they returned despite His authoritative actions.

The first occurred after his first miracle (turning wine into water) and the other after He entered Jerusalem for the last time. John is the only gospel writer who comments on the motivation of the Lord for performing such an audacious act before the people. John's account of the Lord's first cleansing of the temple provides us with the true emotion that Jesus was feeling, and it was not anger!

In John 2:17, after Jesus cleansed the temple, the apostle recorded, "His disciples remembered that it was written, 'Zeal for your house will eat me up.'" The Greek word which is translated "zeal" means "intense feeling, passion, and very strong emotion." It does not mean, nor does it imply anger. This is a direct quote from Psalm 69:9 and the Hebrew word is also translated "zeal," not anger. This word speaks of the passionate devotion and fervor which Jesus possessed.

In numerous other places in the New Testament, the verb form of the Greek word is used to describe Christians who are "fervent in spirit" in their service to the Lord. In Acts 18:25, Luke describes a powerful teacher who debated the Jews named Apollos using this expression, "This man had been instructed in the way of the Lord; and being fervent in spirit, he spoke and taught accurately the things concerning Jesus, although he knew only the baptism of John." Then in Romans 12:11, Paul utilizes the word as he explains various qualities, he desires Christians to possess, "Not lagging in diligence; fervent in spirit; serving the Lord." In Revelation 3:15, it is used in its adjectival form when Jesus accused the church of Laodicea of not being cold or hot (zealous) for the Lord but only lukewarm. The Lord Jesus said, "I know your works, that you are neither cold nor hot. I wish you were cold or hot."

A related verb is utilized in 1 Corinthians 14:1 and 14:39 to speak of the "earnest desire" of the Corinthians to exercise certain spiritual gifts. In 1 Corinthians 14:1, Paul asserts, "Follow after love, and earnestly desire spiritual gifts, but especially that you may prophesy." In 1 Corinthians 14:29, he also declared, "Let the prophets speak, two or three, and let the others discern." The Lord Jesus had so much "fervency in spirit" and "passion" for preserving the purity, holiness, and integrity of God's temple that He was compelled to clear out the money changers on two different occasions. This was done from His authority as the Son of God which is why the apostles never did this.

The disciples were zealous and fervent in spirit for the things of the Father but had no divine authority. On both occasions, the Jewish people questioned His authority to commit such a bold act of rebuke upon them. On the first occasion, they asked for a sign which would demonstrate His divine authority to take such an action. In John 2:18, the apostle writes, ""The Jews therefore answered him, 'What sign do you show us, seeing that you do these things?'" On the second occasion, they demanded a verbal response from the Lord. In Matthew 21:23, Matthew records it this way, "When he had come into the temple, the chief priests and the elders of the people came to him as he was teaching, and said, 'By what authority do you do these things? Who gave you this authority?'" This cleansing required real authority.

There is one incident that the usual word for anger in the Greek language (not this word) is used of Jesus which can be found in the account of the restoration of a man's withered hand in the temple on the Sabbath. In Mark 3:5, Mark writes that Jesus was angry and sorrowful at their hardened hearts. Neither had been directed at them personally but instead at their hardened hearts.

The passage reads thus, "When he had looked around at them with anger, being grieved at the hardening of their hearts, he said to the man, 'Stretch out your hand.' He stretched it out, and his hand was restored as healthy as the other.'" As this powerful miracle occurred, several Jewish leaders were watching. They taught that there was to be no working on the Sabbath. In their minds, "healing" someone was basically working; therefore, there was to be no healing on this holy day! They were adamant about this.

Amid this display of their ignorance, Mark described the two emotions our Lord Jesus experienced at this moment: anger and grief. Neither was directed at them personally but at their hardened hearts. He was angry and sorrowful that their hearts could become so calloused that they would not allow the Son of God to show compassion on a man who had suffered such a great malady.

The Lord felt angry and sorrowful that their rules, which they thought were God's rules, were so utterly far from His Father's true ways. They actually thought that in their cold, calculated, and hardened hearts that they were serving the living and true God. Yet, they knew nothing of His Father! Though the feelings were there, they never issued forth in evil thoughts toward these lost souls, evil words of cursing, or even evil actions of violence.

So, what then is the Scriptural principle? The key truth that should guide us in the taming of our tempers is "we must put away all anger in our relationships." Our natural feelings of anger might often be prevented, must always be managed, and their expression in our thoughts, words, and deeds must be eliminated. This is a life-changing distinction.

When our natural feelings of anger arise, they may never express themselves in angry thoughts, words, or actions. There is absolutely no place in relationships where anger produces positive effects; they are always negative. Though some people may suggest that it is a wonderful idea to "fight something out," this does not work and is never God's way; therefore, it is definitely not something we should become engaged in. The fiery blaze of our tempers must always be extinguished. There is no other option allowed.

Workbook Questions

Directions: Now that you have read this chapter, answer the following questions. Answers to the questions regarding the text can be found in chapter nine.

1. According to John 2:17, why can we not use the example of Jesus cleansing the temple to justify righteous anger?

2. According to the author, why did Jesus cleanse the temple, but the apostles did not?

3. According to Mark 3:5, what actually made Jesus angry and sad in the one incident recorded?

4. According to the author, what are two reasons we should not "fight an argument out?"

5. According to the author, what is the Scriptural principle in his words?

6. How would you express the principle in your own words?

7. How would you rewrite this principle to make it even more personal to your life (using your name and situation)?

8. Why do you think this principle might be important in your life right now?

9. How would you rate yourself on the percentage of times you followed the Scriptural principle in the past when you were annoyed?

Directions: Put a horizontal mark and your name where you see yourself on the percentage line.

| 0% | 25% | 50% | 75% | 100% |

Chapter 3

Controlling the Heat:
A Biblical Explanation

Once the fire has started, how do we control the heat of
our tempers that are blazing? We must start with a proper
understanding of what aspects of anger are sinful and which
are not. Let's begin with the teaching of the Lord Jesus. The
instruction concerning anger in God's Holy Word would
have been extremely clear to Him. Jesus knew the Scriptures
and that any expression of anger was forbidden by the Lord
God. In fact, Jesus also taught this same truth. It was a heart
violation of the sixth commandment which clearly states,
"You shall not murder" (Exodus 20:13; Deuteronomy 5:17).
The Ten Commandments did not have to do with outward
actions alone but also the heart. They governed all thoughts,
words, and actions. The Lord's general discussion is found
in Matthew chapter five.

In Matthew 5:21-24, Jesus condemned anger as murder of
the heart as He addressed the true heart intent of the sixth
commandment. When our tempers issue forth into angry
thoughts, words, or any actions (short of murder), these are
also sins of "murder" but "murder of the heart." Jesus states,
"But I tell you, that everyone who is angry with his brother
will be in danger of the judgment [sinful]; and whoever says
to his brother, 'Raca!' will be in danger of the council [sinful];
and whoever says, 'You fool!' will be in danger of the fire of
Gehenna" (DEJ). According to the Lord, a person cannot be
angry with his brother (in thoughts), and then say, "Raca" or
"You fool" (in words). Also, murder (in actions) is implied.
Since our words are less violent than actions and are sins,
then harmful actions from a murderous heart are also sins.

Paul continues to elucidate God's truth concerning anger. He teaches this principle clearly from two different passages. In Ephesians 4:31, the apostle commands, "Let all bitterness, wrath, anger, outcry, and slander, be put away from you, with all malice." In Colossians 3:8, he then repeats, "But now you also put them all away: anger, wrath, malice, slander, and shameful speaking out of your mouth." Paul uses two different words in his similar commands. We are to remove our anger. The word translated "wrath" refers to a quick-tempered rage and "anger" is more the general idea. Both are condemned. We should remove them. This is taught in the Old Testament as well. In Psalm 37:8, King David urges his readers, "Cease from anger, and forsake wrath. Don't fret." Here he utilizes the three Hebrew terms which designate general anger, quick tempered wrath, and even hot rage respectively. Then the inspired writer commands us to cease, forsake and don't act on them. Why? As we saw, "It leads only to evildoing." The inspired writers and our Lord agree that anger is to be "put away" when it wells up inside us.

Of course, the question then arises, "What about feelings of anger, are they also sinful?" Sometimes, we feel angry. It comes on suddenly without forethought. One minute we are calm and peaceful and another minute, we are angry and bitter. How can this be sinful or wrong? Paul answers these two critical questions in his discussion of anger in Ephesians 4:26-27. He commands, "'Be angry, and don't sin. Don't let the sun go down on your wrath, and don't give place to the devil." The Greek word translated "be angry" is the standard word for general anger. He's speaking of all anger with its many facets and nuances.

Now, to take this reference to the next level, let's take a moment for a simple Greek grammar lesson. This verb "be angry" is in the present passive imperative tense. It conveys three crucial meanings. First, the verb "be angry" is in the "imperative," which means it is a command. Second, it is present tense. This denotes continuous action in present time. This means that the anger does not just arise and leave as fast as it came, it could stay awhile, or it could come back. It might stay because they need more time to process the anger. It may come back because the situation returns and triggers again. Third, the word is in the passive voice which indicates that the anger has been instigated by an outside source. The person is becoming angry because something has actively come upon him, and his temper is aroused. Something from outside the person is prompting the inward feeling. The angry feelings are on the inside, but someone or something is provoking or stirring it up on the outside. It comes upon a person without their volition. They do not make a conscious decision to get angry, it happens to them.

The apostle Paul recognizes the fact that Christians may become angry without premeditation, and the feelings may come upon them suddenly. The feelings of anger are not the sin; it is what they do with the angry feelings that are the sin. To put it another way, feeling angry is not sinful; it is the manifestation of those feelings of anger in thoughts, words, and deeds that is sin. This is a critical distinction.

Now, there are three ways in which the feelings of anger can be sinful because they come from within not without. This would be the word in the active voice. We instigate this. Let me explain. The first can occur when we dwell on the incident and allow our anger and tempers to grow. The Bible calls this process "churning our anger." In Proverbs 30:33, King Solomon absolutely advised against this action, "For as the churning of milk produces butter, and the wringing of the nose produces blood; so, the forcing of wrath produces strife." We can churn what happened within our hearts like one makes butter by continuously thinking angry thoughts about the person. This makes our soft hearts become hard

17

and bitter toward the other person. We can think about it over and over while our nostrils are flaring in anger, but it produces conflict with the other person and strife within us.

We can spend nights planning revenge against the person turning our angry feelings into a raging fire. In Hosea 7:6, the prophet describes evil men in these words, "For they have prepared their heart like an oven, while they lie in wait plotting. Their anger smolders all night, in the morning it burns like a flaming fire" (DEJ). We can let the fire within us smolder all night until it explodes into horrendous words and actions from our evil plotting. Both of these passages teach the ruminating of anger as sin. So, dwelling on the feelings of the anger are sinful because now it is inside us. When the next incident occurs, it flares right up because it had never been put off or carried away.

The second way in which feelings can become sinful is to become angry so often that we develop the habit of anger. This anger comes from within us not from without as Paul is discussing. Sometimes, we become angry because we have developed a habit of angry outbursts. We have allowed our temper to be unleashed so often that it becomes our "go to" response whenever things do go our way or people disagree with us.

This is usually referred to as being quick-tempered. This will cause our "angry feelings" to become an integral part of ourselves because we have "nurtured" them to the point of practicing anger. The feelings do not come upon us from the outside, but it is a habit that arises immediately from within ourselves when an incident occurs. It may be sudden due to the particular trigger, but it doesn't come upon us passively.

Why? It has been practiced by us all along. In Galatians 5, Paul contrasts the fruits of the Spirit we produce when we walk in the Spirit with the deeds of the flesh we practice when we walk in the flesh. In verses 19-21, the apostle pens these words, "Now the deeds of the flesh are obvious, which are: adultery, sexual immorality, uncleanness, lustfulness, idolatry, sorcery, hatred, strife, jealousies, outbursts of anger [actions of an untamed temper], rivalries, divisions, heresies, envy, murders, drunkenness, orgies, and things like these; of which I forewarn you, even as I also forewarned you, that those who practice [continually] such things will not inherit God's Kingdom." Notice here, the apostle uses the word "practice" with "outbursts of anger." He is speaking here of the habitual expression of our untamed tempers. These are deeds of the flesh and must be removed and replaced with the fruits of the Spirit, such as "patience" (Galatians 5:22).

In Ephesians 4:22, he addresses this same issue from a different perspective. Paul asserts, "That you put away, as concerning your former way of life, the old man, that grows corrupt after the lusts of deceit." Here, the apostle refers to our lives before knowing Christ as our "former way." This way or manner in which we lived must now be "put away." Would this not include the practice of angry outbursts as well as the outbursts themselves as in Galatians 5? The New Testament writers spoke of many habits which did not honor God (1 Timothy 5:13; Hebrews 10:25). Developing a habit of responding in anger to what displeases us would belong in this group of unrighteous habits.

The third is the enjoyment of getting angry and letting our tempers flare. This also comes from within and not without. In Galatians 5:24, after Paul mentions of the deeds of the flesh, one of which is "outbursts of anger," he writes, "Those who belong to Christ have crucified the flesh with its passions and lusts." These outbursts of anger can be enjoyed as an expression of our passion and lust. We can lust after the moments where we can experience the full passion of our raging anger. These also come from within and are sinful. If we enjoy becoming angry then when our lust of anger is incited, those feelings can also become sinful.

As was mentioned, Christians are to remove the feelings of anger and instead replace them with patience and self-control. As believers, we are able to get our anger under control and not express it through the power of the Holy Spirit. This is spiritual patience. In Galatians 5:22-23, Paul describes the Spirit's work in these words, "But the fruit of the Spirit is love, joy, peace, patience, kindness, goodness, faith, gentleness, and self-control." Notice, Paul mentions those very words (patience and self-control) which are truly important in dealing with our temper, anger, and wrath. It is self-control which helps us in "controlling the heat of our tempers and respond patiently instead. The fruits should replace the fiery inferno and blaze. How does this happen? This is often not instantaneous but more of a process which we will discuss in the next chapter.

Workbook Questions

Directions: Now that you have read this chapter, answer the following questions. Answers to the questions regarding the text can be found in chapter nine.

1. According to Jesus, what commandment is broken when we express our anger (with Bible verses)?

2. According to Jesus, how is the expression of our anger a kind of "murder?"

3. According to Matthew 5:21-24, what expressions of anger are actual sins?

4. According to Ephesians 4:32 and Colossians 3:8, what are Christians supposed to do with their angry feelings?

5. According to Psalm 37:8, what is the eventual result of all expressions of anger?

6. According to Ephesians 4:26, what aspect of our anger is not a sin?

7. According to Paul's use of the term "anger," what would be three qualities of this anger which is not sinful?

8. According to the author, what is the first way that feelings can actually be sinful (provide the Bible verses)?

9. According to the author, what is the second way that feelings can actually be sinful (provide the Bible verses)?

10. According to the author, what is the third way that feelings can actually be sinful (provide the Bible verses)?

11. According to Galatians 5:22-23, what fruit of the Spirit should we express rather than anger?

12. In what ways have these truths impacted your life and relationships?

Chapter 4

Stomping Out the Fire: A Godly Technique

In this chapter, we will discuss godly techniques to help us stomp the fire of our tempers out. I am using the analogy of fire because it is easy to think of our anger as a ball of fire in our inner hearts. When Solomon speaks of the problem of pursuing after lust, he uses the analogy of fire. In Proverbs 6:27, Solomon asked, "Can a man scoop fire into his bosom, and his clothes not be scorched?" (DEJ). Then in Proverbs 29:8, Solomon utilizes the fire analogy for the devastation that one's anger can bring. It sets a city on fire. He explains, "Mockers set a city on fire, but wise men turn away anger" (DEJ).

As we have seen in Galatians 5:20, "outbursts of anger" proceed from the lusts of the flesh. So, let us think of our feelings of anger as a ball of fire that might well up in us and could be thrown at other people through our angry thoughts pouring forth in harsh words and evil deeds. So, do we, as Christians, continually stoke and fuel the fire or constantly stomp them out? It depends on what we decide to do.

We can immediately throw that ball of fire at the people who have transgressed us and destroy the relationships we have with them. Or we can extinguish the fire God's way. The Lord's method of dealing with anger is to "put it away" or "put it off." These were mentioned briefly; now, let's take a closer look at both. In Ephesians 4:31, he uses the first term and in Colossians 3:8, Paul utilizes the second term. Both describe this process. The Greek word which is translated "put it away" means to remove it or take it away." The Greek word for "put it off" refers to putting off an article of clothing or putting something aside. We should put away or take off the anger that we might be feeling. In our analogy, we need to take action to stomp out the fire that has been created.

Although Paul does not provide the exact process himself, it would have been very familiar to the Jewish saints from because David speaks of it in the Old Testament. The process is alluded to in his injunction found in Ephesians 4:26, "Be angry, but do not sin." This Greek phrase is utilized in the Hebrew in Psalm 4:4 by King David. In this dramatic psalm, David is angry. Many opponents have risen against him, and he cries out to the Lord in prayer for relief. As he describes his anguish, he turns his attention to his future readers and explains what to do when one becomes angry.

In Psalm 4:4, he writes, "Tremble, and do not sin; meditate upon your bed, and be still. Selah" (DEJ). Here David speaks of trembling in anger because his enemies are spreading lies about him. He is so angry that his whole body is trembling. Have you ever felt that way? We all have. At times, we may become so angry that we begin to tremble. Here, David uses the extreme to encompass any anger that is about to express itself. Yet, we may never sin in thoughts, words, or actions. When this fire has welled up in us to the point of trembling, what do we do with it?

Step #1: Separate Yourself

First, we go to our bed. Though this might sound strange with careful consideration, it makes perfect sense. They lived in a Bedouin world of tents. Like our bedrooms of today, the room with the "bed" would be separate from the other rooms by a covering. This would be the only place someone could be alone. He does not mean to literally go to our beds but to remove ourselves from the situation which is provoking the anger. We might call it today taking a "time out." We leave the situation provoking our rage and the people who we are about to explode upon, if at all possible.

In the Old Testament book of Second Kings, the prophet Elisha is continually predicting every move that Syria makes in its war with Israel and warning them. In 2 Kings 6:12, the writer portrays the exasperation of one of the king's servants in these words, "One of his servants said, 'No, my lord, O king; but Elisha, the prophet who is in Israel, tells the king of Israel the words that you speak in your bedroom." How could Elisha have heard the words that were spoken in the most isolated of places? They were dumbfounded, but we know that God was revealing the words to him. So, the bed was considered a place where one could be alone. It was a place of solitude.

Let me put it this way, "We must leave the scene of the crime." Our bed is a quiet spot away from the provocation. It fits perfectly with Paul's injunction to "put it or take it away." We literally take the fireball of our flaming temper away from the situation to a quiet, restful place. The Hebrew word translated "bed" also has the connotation of "lying down." This word conveys the idea of resting and relaxing.

In Job 7:13-14, Job complains to God because of his many nightmares due to pain. Notice how he describes the bed for him, "When I say, 'My bed shall comfort me. My couch shall ease my complaint. Then you scare me with dreams and terrify me through visions.'" It is to bring rest and comfort, not torment. In Isaiah 57:2, the prophet describes righteous people as resting in their beds, "He enters into peace. They rest in their beds, each one who walks in his uprightness." So, to stomp out the fire of our tempers we must separate ourselves from the incident that is fueling it.

Step #2: Talk Yourself Down

Second, Christians should "meditate." Biblical meditation is nothing like what is seen in the world. The Hebrew word "meditate" literally means "to speak or talk." It carries the idea of talking things over with ourselves and God. We mull things over in our minds and add God's input from His Word. So, we are talking the whole situation over with God through prayer and the Word. We are attempting to tame out tempers by acknowledging that God does not want our anger expressed. This will not glorify Him and will only destroy relationships in the process.

During this time, we should pray for wisdom (James 1:5) and search the Scriptures (Psalm 119:50), if necessary. It is through these powerful tools that we can subdue our anger and renew a biblical perspective. Also, during this time, we should follow Paul's injunction in Ephesians 4:22-24. Though we have discussed the first portion, the second pertains here. The apostle declares this, "That you put away, as concerning your former way of life, the old man, that grows corrupt after the lusts of deceit."

Here is the removal of our old unbelieving ways (anger and bitterness). Then the apostle continues, "And that you be renewed in the spirit of your mind." This important time of meditation works on the mind to see things God's way. It is renewed in the Holy Spirit working through His Word. Paul finishes this passage with the new response, "And put on the new man, who in the likeness of the Lord has been created in righteousness and holiness of truth."

The Greek word which is translated "new" means "brand new of a different kind." Christians put on the completely new and divine response of patience and self-control. These character traits distinguish believers as they follow God.

Step #3: Release Your Anger

While we are involved in this process, David explains the next step, "Be still." Stop everything else. All of our thoughts, words, and actions come to a halt. Our body stops. We stop and take the necessary time to process the situation in our minds. This important word also carries the sense of relaxing and releasing something. He is saying, "Calm down and let it go." This Hebrew word translated "be still" can also mean "be silent, still, wait." In Psalm 37:8, the psalmist helps us with this concept when he says, "Cease from anger and forsake wrath. Don't fret, it leads to evildoing." The word "cease" is a very powerful Hebrew word. The word means to "drop and relax." We drop the matter, let the issue go, and completely relax in our decision to follow God.

We can rest in the Lord's power and sovereignty to work the issue out. In Psalm 62:1, the Psalmist peacefully utters, "My soul rests in God alone. My salvation is from him." Then in verse, 5-6, he writes, "My soul, wait in silence for God alone." This waiting is for our Father God to prepare all the hearts involved including our own to resolve the issue rather than exacerbate it. Then he adds the perspective we should have, "For my expectation is from him. He alone is my rock and my salvation, my fortress. I will not be shaken." Then, a calmness should fill our hearts as we relinquish all of difficulty to Him and rely on His power.

In Psalm 131:2, the psalmist writes, "Surely I have stilled and quieted my soul, like a weaned child with his mother." A child who is not weaned depends upon his mother to sustain him. One who is weaned leans upon his mother for comfort and support. This is a time of resting in God. Then, there is a "Selah" which was a Hebrew pause in a song. It is as if David is saying, "Please pause and contemplate what I just said." So, release it. How does that translate into life?

If our own wives, children, parents, friends, neighbors, or bosses provoke us to anger, we ought to realize we are getting upset and separate ourselves, talk ourselves down, and release our anger. Essentially, we need to leave the situation and meditate until we have calmed down. The resolution of any problem cannot come in the heat of anger. If we do not get angry but the other party does, then we must take the initiative and tell them we both need a time out. We should never engage their anger. We might say, "I think it's time I took a time out or excuse me for just a moment!" Then, we walk away. If the situation dictates, we repeat ourselves once and then leave. The Lord God does not want His children quarreling for any reason (Proverbs 20:3; 2 Timothy 2:24).

Step #4: Ask for Forgiveness

Before we can resolve the conflict that caused the anger, we must reconcile the relationship by asking for forgiveness. In Matthew 5, the Lord discusses the various heart attitudes people in His kingdom should not possess. After speaking of anger, the Lord presents a general principle of living in His kingdom on Earth. In verses 23-24, He explains, "If therefore you are offering your gift at the altar, and there remember that your brother has anything against you, leave your gift there before the altar, and go your way.

First be reconciled to your brother, and then come and offer your gift." The Greek word translated "reconciled" means "to make changes." It originates from a Greek root word that was a banking term meaning to "render accounts the same." There would be a discrepancy between two bank ledgers. Then, they would have to find the mistakes and fix them, so both were the same. We express this as "being on the same page." Before we can resolve, we must reconcile.

The Lord indicates that God desires His people to come to Him fully reconciled with each other. If we, as Christians, know that someone harbors something against us, or even we have done something to them, we take the initiative and go to them and reconcile with them. We should not wait for them to come to us. We take our responsibility and go to them. We must once again "settle accounts." We allowed our tempers to flare, so we should humble ourselves and ask for forgiveness.

The asking of forgiveness is both obvious and natural. In Luke 17:3-4, Jesus states, "Be careful. If your brother sins against you, rebuke him. If he repents, forgive him. If he sins against you seven times in the day, and seven times returns, saying, 'I repent,' you shall forgive him." In this passage, Jesus presupposes that someone will repent. The "repenting" implies that the other asks for forgiveness. When we have unleashed our anger upon others, we intuitively know that we ought to repent and ask for forgiveness because we are convicted by our consciences (Romans 2:15).

Step #5: Forgive Yourself

The next step we should take is to forgive ourselves for our angry outburst. Though obvious, this is often difficult. We must forgive ourselves for our sin as God has forgiven us. If we do not, we will feel defeated, broken, and unable to build the relationship anew. We do not have to carry this burden; instead, we can be free of it once and for all. The best method in doing this is to review how God has forgiven our sins.

In Colossians 2:13-14, Paul explains how God has nailed our sins and their resultant judgment which he calls "debts" to the cross of Jesus Christ, "You were dead through your trespasses and the uncircumcision of your flesh. He made you alive together with him, having forgiven us all our trespasses, wiping out the handwriting in ordinances which was against us; and he has taken it out of the way, nailing it to the cross." We must tell ourselves that Christ shed His blood to take its judgment on our behalf.

There are many analogies used of God removing our sin from us. He has concealed, hidden, and covered over our sin (Psalm 85:2). The Lord God has stomped out the sins of our angry words and actions. He has also thrown them into the depths of the sea (Micah 7:19). God, the Almighty has cast the wickedness of and sin our untamed tempers behind His back because He refuses to see it (Isaiah 38:17). In His great compassion, God has blotted out our raging until it is no more (Isaiah 43:25). Our merciful and gracious Father has forgotten our outrages (Hebrews 8:12).

All of this occurred because of what His Son Jesus Christ did on the cross for you. In Isaiah 1:18, God says to Israel that, "though your sins be as scarlet, they shall be as white as snow." God has washed away this iniquity and now we are glistening in the sun (Son) as the whitest of snow. It is over, and we must move on to the restoring the relationship. We cannot resolve the conflicts we may have with others until we restore the relationships with them.

Step #6: Restore the Relationship

The next step is to rebuild the relationship. How can we resolve the conflict which instigated the anger when the bond between us has been broken? We must mend it. In Galatians 6:1, Paul explains this important concept when he exhorts the many saints in the city, "Brothers, even if a man is caught in some fault, you who are spiritual must restore such a one in a spirit of gentleness." Here, Paul is speaking of someone who is caught in a sin and the other believers help restore them. If the sin is only against God, they repent and accept His forgiveness. If others have been sinned against, then they must do the same with them.

Untamed tempers destroy relationships, and they need to be restored. The Greek word which is translated "restore" can mean "to render fit, sound, or complete; to mend or repair what has been broken; to equip and prepare someone for something; to complete." In this context, it means to mend or repair what was broken. The Greek word is used of a physically broken fishing net. In Mark 1:19 and Matthew 4:21, when Jesus called James and John into ministry with Him, they were in the process of "mending" their fishing nets. They were removing the holes in their net that would allow the fish to fall through. These soon-to-be disciples were sewing it up so to speak.

When a relationship has been broken, it must always be mended. All the holes must be patched and repaired so the relationship is whole again. How does this happen? What do we actually do to mend the relationship? It is through the utilization of many loving words and actions. These words and actions rebuild relationships in the same way as they were used to build them in the first place.

In Revelation 2, Jesus accuses the believers in Ephesus of falling out of love with Him. In verse 5, He explains what is needed, "Remember therefore from where you have fallen, and repent and do the first works." Jesus simply commands them to repent which is the "asking for forgiveness" we just discussed. Then, He tells them to do "the first works" which refer to the deeds they did when they first received Him as Savior and Lord and loved Him for it. Notice, Christ does not mention any feelings but actions. No matter how we may feel inside, to restore a relationship, we should treat the relationship as if it were new and fresh. Once this is done, we should speak the words and take the actions which built it in the first place.

How do we find the motivation to do it? This is found in the first part of verse 5. We remember what it was like in the beginning when we were in love with each other. When we do this, it does not matter what their response will be or whether we feel the desire to do it. If we do not feel the desire to do it, we can feel the desire to obey God in an act of obedience and have the faith that He will work both in the person's heart and in ours. So, we launch into the beginning deeds. We should expect the previous feelings to return in time. Normally, this will be to their previous level. If we continue to do these deeds, then we may actually increase the feelings and bring them to a higher level.

If the feelings do not return and the deeds are being done with good intentions on our part, then it is time to pray for divine intervention on both our parts. This will require effort on both sides, and this does not always happen. If we have a true open heart and the willingness to exert needed effort, then we must rely on the Holy Spirit to do the rest. Once we have reconciled and restored the relationships through the steps I described, we then proceed to resolving the issue the actual conflict at hand.

Step #7 - Resolve the Conflict

When our anger is calmed, we must resolve the situation that caused it in the first place. This is a necessary next step. It is important that we distinguish the angry response from the problem itself. Dealing with the angry response will not solve the problem. As long as the situation that instigated the angry response has not been settled, the embers of our anger will still be smoldering waiting once again to be fueled from the same situation arising. This cannot always happen because we may be unable to let the anger go long enough to really discuss it with the other person.

So, the next best approach would be the setting up of a time to resolve the issue. The appointment will help calm the situation. Of course, this will require a trust by both parties that a fair discussion of the problem will occur. At this point, both partners must realize that arguing and fighting as a way of resolving any issue only adds additional problems. So, it is best to make a commitment to resolve the issue as soon as possible after the anger has subsided. This way, both parties can work on the anger first.

In Ephesians 4:26, Paul states, "'Be angry, and don't sin.' Don't let the sun go down on your wrath." The word "wrath" is a different word than Paul used in the first part of the verse. Here, the apostle is focusing on the instigation of the anger. Paul stipulates that it should be done before the sun goes down. We should not go to bed angry. If we cannot deal with it at the moment, we should set a time or make an appointment for a full discussion to resolve it when those involved are calm.

There are two methods to resolve the conflict: cover over the incident in love or take it to a decision-making process. Now, whether one method or another should be utilized depends on how important it is to the parties. If it can be covered over in love by both parties, then it should be. If either party cannot do this, it must be dealt with through the decision-making process. We will discuss this briefly.

The first principle in resolving conflicts is to cover over the less important issues in love. In Proverbs 10:12 it says,

"Hatred stirs up strife, but love covers all wrongs." The parallel passage is found in 1 Peter 4:8, "And above all things be earnest in your love among yourselves, for love covers a multitude of sins." Both Solomon and Peter wrote of the importance of covering over many sins in love. These two passages describing the same concept unveil the secret to long lasting relationships. Our love should cover over the small annoyances, minor irritations, and often, even the greater transgressions that might occur as we interact in our various relationships with people. The word translated "cover" means to "cover over, conceal, or hide." When we love others, we should really conceal the smaller problems between us and others by letting them go and not even mentioning them at all.

Now, how do we cover over something in love? After an incident occurs that arouses our anger, we reassess our love and commitment to the person and then "decide" to cover over the problem. We should ask ourselves this question, "Do I love this person?" If the answer comes back in the affirmative, then we decide that this issue is not important enough to even take a chance of destroying even a small portion of what we have together. Then, we let it go for the greater good of us both. We simply release the issue.

Unfortunately, other issues are too big to cover over. This brings us to the second principle which is to decide together on the larger issues in unity. The biblical decision-making process has several critical steps which I will only mention. First, we should seek God's will under the Lordship of Christ (Romans 12:11). We should recognize His presence as we work out the issue. Second, the decisions that are made should be in unity (Philippians 2:1-2). Third, there should be a careful search of the Scriptures for the biblical principles that govern a situation (Acts 17:11). Fourth, we should pray for wisdom as we study (James 1:5). Fifth, we should be coming to the process to follow the Lord's will, not our own selfish pleasures and desires (1 Corinthians 10:24).

Sixth, we should examine every detail carefully and then suggest the various courses of holy action God may desire for us to take (1 Thessalonians 5:21-22). Seventh, both need to listen to the others involved (James 1:19). Eighth, the parties involved should carefully assess the impact of the solutions which come to mind on everyone who is involved (Acts 15:6-29). Ninth, we must be willing to sacrifice and compromise for the good of all (Philippians 2:3-4). Tenth, if we should seek wise counsel (Proverbs 11:14). Eleventh, we should continue the process until we have fully decided on a course of action (1 Corinthians 1:10). Twelfth, if this cannot be done, we should find a Christian mediator to aid us in the process (1 Corinthians 6:1-7). Once we resolve some of the important issues of conflict in the relationship, it will be much more unified and even fulfilling. Many issues in the relationships are nothing more than a series of conflicts that have never been resolved.

Now, when it comes to the serious, long-term practice of sins (drunkenness, pornography, gambling, etc.), then these cannot be overlooked or may not be able to be dealt with in a decision making process; instead, the church, professionals who specialize, or even law may have to become involved (Matthew 18:15-18; Romans 12:1-4; 1 Corinthians 6:1-5).

Step #8 - Prepare for Battle

All of these processes will prevent an opportunity for the Devil to destroy our relationships. In Ephesians 4:27, Paul concludes his thought with these words, "And do not give place to the Devil." The word translated "give" means "to reach out the hand to furnish." The word translated "place" means "a portion or space marked off for a specific purpose, or an occasion for acting on something." An untamed temper reaches out our hands to the Devil to provide him with a specially marked off spot in our relationships to destroy them.

Remember what Peter warned his readers concerning the Devil. In 1 Peter 5:8, he describes it this way, "Be sober and self-controlled. Be watchful. Your adversary, the devil, walks around like a roaring lion, seeking whom he may devour." He is a starving lion prowling and trolling for his prey. Our tempers will throw him the meat he desires.

We also can't let our enemy within have an opportunity. When we become angry or have developed an angry habit or bad temper, we must realize that we may have to battle ourselves to eliminate the angry expression and tame our feelings. Why? As I mentioned earlier, we have a serious enemy within which resides in our bodies. In Romans 7:23, Paul describes his battle with the flesh, "But I see a different law in my members [flesh], warring against the law of my mind, and bringing me into captivity [battle] under the law of sin which is in my members." The "different law in my members" refers to a "law" that rules our physical body. This is called the "flesh."

It resides in the physical body and prompts and incites us to become angry rather than patient. In Galatians 5:16, Paul explains what to do, "But I say, walk by the Spirit, and you won't fulfill the lust of the flesh." Here, Paul indicates that the best way to tame the flesh (thereby our tempers) is to "walk by the Spirit." We must build up divinely powerful, supernatural strength to resist our lusts to follow the Spirit.

How is this possibly done? It is primarily through God's two strength builders: the Bible and prayer. Paul explains the power of God's Word in his letter to the Thessalonian church. Paul had only been in Thessalonica a short time, but the gospel (God's Word) had a powerful effect on these believers. In 1 Thessalonians 1:5, Paul writes this, "And that our Good News came to you not in word only but also in power, and in the Holy Spirit, and with much assurance. You know what kind of men we showed ourselves to be among you for your sake." Among these new believers, the gospel came in word (this is what we read), and in power (as we live it), and in the Holy Spirit (as He enables us).

The Greek word which is translated "power," is the Greek root word from which we get our English word "dynamite." It speaks of explosive and mighty power. And this power is the power of deity; it is supernatural power. When we read the Word and gain knowledge of God and how he desires us to act, we gain the power to live it out through His Spirit. If we are struggling with the taming of our temper, then a profitable study of the Scriptures might be on this very topic. What do the Scriptures say about expressing God's view on anger and patience? While we are studying God's Word, we must pray for ourselves and all of the others involved. This is so critical to winning the battle. Studying the Word and praying in a specific area can unleash the Spirit's power.

In Ephesians 6:18, Paul describes the importance of prayer in our spiritual battles which does include anger, "With all prayer and requests, praying at all times in the Spirit, and being watchful to this end in all perseverance and requests for all the saints." He encourages the believers to pray as they are alert and watchful. So, regarding our anger, we should be praying for ourselves and also others who may be struggling with taming their temper. As we begin to sense our temper rising or see it in another, we should be alert and pray right then. We can be assured that the Holy Spirit will work if we do battle on our knees.

Step #9 - Fear His Discipline

Next, we must fear God's discipline. In Hebrews 12, the author explains God's discipline process. As a loving father disciplines and trains his children so does God. This refers to God using trials as a tool to help us stop sinning. In verse 11, the author writes, "All chastening seems for the present to be not joyous but grievous; yet afterward it yields the peaceful fruit of righteousness to those who have been exercised thereby." An example of this is found in 1 Corinthians 11, where Paul describes God direct action in stopping the misuse of the Lord's Supper by the saints. In verse 30, it says, "For this cause many among you are weak and sickly, and not a few sleep." Some were sick and weak, and others had been struck dead to stop the abuses among God's people. So, as we attempt to stomp out the fires of our temper, we should have a healthy respect for the fact that God may train us to practice righteousness in being patient. Sometimes, it's the consequences of our sins and other times, it can be the direct hand of God. This is so good for us in the end.

Step #10 - Practice Silence Regularly

Now, there is a critical action that must be taken to allow ourselves the time to handle this ball of fire. It is "silence." We need to restrain our mouths! We need to keep our tongues under control, so the situation can be dealt with properly. If we learn silence, there would be no fires for us to stomp out. In James 1:19-20, James encourages us, "So, then, my beloved brothers, let every man be swift to hear, slow to speak, and slow to anger; for the anger of man doesn't produce the righteousness of God." An additional step might be to practice restraining our words in various situations even when our anger is not provoked. This will aid in our restraining our words when becoming angry. In Proverbs

17:27, Solomon writes of this very issue, "He who spares his words has knowledge. He who is even tempered is a man of understanding." He counseled us to restrain our words. This demonstrates that we are intelligent enough to keep quiet when necessary. The tongue must never let its fire out.

James describes the power of an uncontrolled tongue and the fury it can unleash. In chapter 3 of James, the brother of Jesus utilizes three analogies to express the power of our words: a wild horse, an out-of-control ship, and a raging forest fire. In verses 2-6, he writes, "For in many things we all stumble. If anyone doesn't stumble in word, the same is a perfect man, able to bridle the whole body also. Indeed, we put bits into the horses' mouths so that they may obey us, and we guide their whole body." Here, James explains that we must tame the tongue as we tame a horse. Then he adds this comment, "Behold, the ships also, though they are so big and are driven by fierce winds, are yet guided by a very small rudder, wherever the pilot desires." James speaks of piloting the tongue to control it.

Then he continues, "So the tongue is also a little member, and boasts great things. See how a small fire can spread to a large forest! And the tongue is a fire. The world of iniquity among our members is the tongue, which defiles the whole body, and sets on fire the course of nature, and is set on fire by Gehenna." Now, he asserts that the flames of tongue must be put out. Notice he describes it as seemingly small and insignificant, but it can be used as if it were bursting forth from the very pit of Hell.

As we practice "silence," we will become better able to control our tongues at critical moments in our relationships. If we can develop a habit of caution as we speak, it will be that much easier to hold our tongues when we begin to feel the fireball of anger flame up in our hearts.

Workbook Questions

Directions: Now that you have read this chapter, answer the following questions. Answers to the questions regarding the text can be found in chapter nine.

1. According to Proverbs 6:27; 29:28, what analogy could be used to think of our feelings of anger?

2. According to the author, what does it actually mean to "put away" or "put off" anger?

3. According to Psalm 4:4, what is the first step in dealing with our ball of fire? Why?

4. According to Psalm 4:4, what is the second step and what shall you be doing?

5. According to Psalm 4:4, what is the third step and why is this important?

6. According to Luke 17:3-4, what is the fourth step we should take to reconcile the relationship after unleashing our temper?

7. According to the author, what is step five and what does the Bible say about our sins?

8. According to Galatians 6:1, what does it mean to restore a relationship and how does one do this (Revelation 2:5)?

9. According to Ephesians 4:26, what must be done before the sun sets? If this cannot be accomplished what does the author suggest?

10. According to Proverbs 10:12 and 1 Peter 4:8, how should we handle the smaller transgressions and briefly how would we do it?

11. According to the author, how should we handle most of the larger transgressions and briefly how would we do it?

12. According to Ephesians 4:27 and Romans 7:23 who must we battle and how do we win (the eighth step)?

13. According to Acts 12:11, if we cannot win the battle, who will intervene and how (ninth step)?

14. According to the author we should practice silence (tenth step) regularly. In James 3:2-6, what are three analogies used to describe the tongue and how do we control it?

15. What principles in this chapter were you unfamiliar with, struggled with, and will be able to implement in your life?

Chapter 5

Preventing the Burn:
A Holy Response

In the last chapter, we discussed the response of the angry person to their own anger. Now, we come to responding to the tempers of other people. If someone's fiery temper is blazing in our direction, how can we prevent getting burned? Sometimes, by our actions and words, we may actually fuel the flames and stoke the fire. This never helps because it ignites our own fires, and then we both are raging. Instead, we should react in such a way that we would truly help the person put the fire out. Here are several suggestions from the Scriptures.

Step #1 - Suggest A Time of Separation

First, we respond by asking for a time out. We can leave the angry person to allow them to follow the principles we just discussed. This may mean that we have to literally walk away. Rather than the angry person suggesting a time out, we can. Sometimes, people cannot control themselves and our walking away will defuse the situation immediately. Why? It obviously takes two to argue, quarrel, and fight. In Proverbs 22:24-25, Solomon warns us, "Do not associate with a hot-tempered man; or go with one who harbors anger, you might learn his ways and find a snare for yourself (DEJ)." This is a general principle of living which Solomon provides for God's people. Of course, this cannot always be followed when we have a boss, neighbor, child, parent, or spouse who has a temper that may flare. Yet, if at all possible, we should stop associating with them when they are raging. This will lessen the chance that we will learn their ways by raging ourselves in response or falling into their snare and trap by engaging in the same actions. In extreme cases, we may even have to leave the house while they are raging because they will not leave us alone. We can simply say, "I think we might need a time-out before this escalates to something so much worse. Let's make an appointment right now to discuss it a couple of days from now. I'll be back in a little while when we both have calmed down."

At the times we cannot leave, such as at work or school, we could ask to use the restroom to remove ourselves from the situation for a few minutes. We do not have to deceive them, we can simply say, "I want to continue this discussion, but I would like to use the restroom first." There may be times where we are not able to leave the raging boss, teacher, spouse, parent due to their authority. We may be in a car dealership or at the store and must make a decision, what do we do then? Here are some principles which govern these moments.

Step #2 - Provide A Gentle Response

Second, we should respond with a gentle answer. If we must engage in a discussion of the situation, we ought to respond gently. In Proverbs 15:1, Solomon pens, "A gentle answer turns away wrath, but a harsh word stirs up anger." Then, in Proverbs 25:15, he continues with this adage, "By patience a ruler is persuaded. A soft [gentle] tongue breaks the bone." This wise man explains in the first passage how a gentle response can turn away someone's wrath. It will take "make them retreat" with their fireball of anger aimed at you. Why? In the second passage, Solomon provides one answer: the soft response breaks their bones. It will cause them to feel terribly guilty for their raging because there is such a dramatic contrast between your response and their reaction. Since Proverbs contain general principles of living, these are not hard and fast rules.

Step #3 - Answer with Great Patience

Third, we should also provide a patient answer. This is a "patience" that calms. When the person begins raging, we simply remain calm. In Proverbs 15:18, Solomon asserts this, "A wrathful man stirs up contention, but one who is slow to anger appeases strife." The word "appease" actually means "to quiet." Rather than stir up or instigate the anger, this will defuse the situation. So many times, people fuel another's anger which only leads to a raging fire which destroys. Our patience will make the fire go out.

Step #4 - Maintain the Required Respect

Fourth, we ought always to show respect while speaking. If we respond, it should be done in honor. Though someone may be angry at us, the showing of respect will keep us from engaging in the same behavior. Otherwise, it will cause a back-and-forth retaliation leading to even worse results. In Romans 12:17, Paul commands this, "Repay no one evil for evil. Respect what is honorable in the sight of all men." This mandate encompasses all relationships. In other passages, we find specific relationships discussed. In Ephesians 6:2, he declares, "'Honor your father and mother,' which is the first commandment with a promise." In 1 Timothy 6:1, he writes, "Let as many as are bondservants under the yoke count their own masters worthy of all honor, that the name of God and the doctrine not be blasphemed."

The apostle Peter speaks to this issue also with a general command and then a specific one. In 1 Peter 2:17, he states,

"Honor all men. Love the brotherhood. Fear God. Honor the king." Then in 1 Peter 3:7, he commands, "You husbands, in the same way, live with your wives according to knowledge, giving honor to the woman, as to the weaker vessel, as being also joint heirs of the grace of life; that your prayers may not be hindered." Even though they are acting inappropriately, we cannot do the same. We should always be respectful.

Step #5 - Fully Forgive the Person

Fifth, whether they repent or not, we must fully forgive the angry person as we have been forgiven by God for all our sins. This will not be easy and is a supernatural, divine act. This forgiveness process is not dependent on others asking for the forgiveness first, making restitution, or even accepting the consequences. In the following passages, our forgiveness is not contingent upon these three actions by the transgressor. These three actions rebuild relationships rather than being conditions for forgiveness. True believers simply forgive as God has forgiven them. In the following passages, Jesus does not add conditions to his commands to forgive.

The Lord taught this principle throughout His ministry. In Matthew 6:12, He taught the disciples to pray, "Forgive us our debts, as we also forgive our debtors." In Mark 11:25, the Lord told Peter, "Whenever you stand praying, forgive, if you have anything against anyone." In Luke 11:4, Jesus repeated His important model for prayer which concluded with these words, "Forgive us our sins, for we ourselves also forgive everyone who is indebted to us." Notice, Jesus makes no distinctions between whether the transgressors must be believers or unbelievers in forgiveness. All must be forgiven because Jesus uses the inclusive terms, "debtors," "anyone," and "everyone." Those who may have difficulty controlling their anger towards us are to be forgiven.

As we can see, we will have a choice when others direct their fiery tempers toward us. Do we throw fuel on their fires and start our own in blaze? Or do we respond in a holy manner and prevent both of us from getting burned? We must be prepared beforehand by knowing these responses so we can choose the holy response.

Workbook Questions

Directions: Now that you have read this chapter, answer the following questions. Answers to the questions regarding the text can be found in chapter nine.

1. According to the author, what is step one?

2. According to Proverbs 22:24-25, what may happen if we continually engaged in another's anger toward us?

3. According to Proverbs 15:1 and Proverbs 15:18, in what way should we answer the angry person if we cannot leave (step two)?

4. According to Proverbs 15:18, in what critical way should we answer the angry person if we cannot leave (step three)?

5. According to Romans 12:17, what is step four and why is it important?

6. According to the author's discussion of step five, is our forgiveness of someone who unleashed their anger on us dependent upon their repentance and why?

7. According to the Lord Jesus, who should be forgiven and who should not if they transgressed us? (Provide verses)

8. What principles in this chapter were you unfamiliar with, struggled with, and will be able to implement in your life?

9. Are there other principles from the Scriptures which you think should be included?

Chapter 6

Fanning the Flame: An Ancient Portrait

In 1 Samuel 13 to 2 Samuel 21, the Scriptures provide an example of how King Saul fanned the flames of his temper when he became jealous of David. He refused to put away his anger and desired revenge and David was patient and sought reconciliation. This is the story of a conflict between Saul and David, the first and second kings of Israel.

The author indicates that an evil spirit began to torment Saul. The king's advisers suggested that a righteous man named David come and play the harp to console him and ease the anguish. This was the same David that had just been anointed by Samuel and he knew it, but they did not.

In 1 Samuel 16:18, they described David in these critical words, "Then one of the young men answered, and said, 'Behold, I have seen a son of Jesse the Bethlehemite who is skillful in playing, a mighty man of valor, a man of war, prudent in speech, and a handsome person; and Yahweh is with him.'" He was a man as distinguished as Saul himself, though not yet known by the people. So, young David was called to play music to soothe Saul's pain, whenever he was tormented. At first, Saul loved David and made him his personal armor bearer. So, when Saul went out to battle, he depended on David to carry additional weapons and to protect him if needed. Then one day, a giant named Goliath appeared.

The Philistines stood on one mountain and the powerful army of Israel on the other. Between them was a valley. Into that valley walked an enormous Philistine warrior (a giant of a man). His name was Goliath. He challenged the Israelites to produce just one man to engage in combat with him. The army of the loser of the battle would surrender and become slaves of the other one. The response of the Israelites was nothing less than absolute horror!

In 1 Samuel 17:11, the writer describes their frightened reaction, "When Saul and all Israel heard those words of the Philistine, they were dismayed, and greatly afraid." The Hebrew word translated "dismayed" means "shattered or broken." In the Hebrew the word translated "afraid" means "astonished or awestruck terror." This author described them as "greatly" afraid. This Hebrew word translated "greatly" means "excessively or abundantly." This mighty army had never seen a man like him. They were terribly afraid. When David approached the battlefield to bring some food to his brothers, he discovered that this arrogant monster of a man was taunting the great armies of the Lord God.

Since the Lord God had delivered him on so numerous occasions from lions and bears, he would face and defeat this arrogant warrior. With a slingshot and five smooth stones, young David killed this mighty giant of a man. It was over quickly in God's power.

From that day forward, Saul would not let David go back home. Saul wanted this young warrior in his service right away. Saul's son Jonathon and David became extremely close friends. King Saul set David over his entire army, and this warrior won battle after battle. After each of these victories, the young women would stand outside with their tambourines and other musical instruments to celebrate the victory. Now they sang, "Saul has slain his thousands, and David his ten thousands." Saul became very jealous, and his anger was aroused. In 1 Samuel 18:8-9, it is described this way, "Saul was very angry, and this saying displeased him. He said, 'They have ascribed to David ten thousands, and to me they have ascribed only thousands. What can he have more but the kingdom?' King Saul watched David from that day forward."

Now here is the anger we have been discussing. Saul and David had a close relationship and David, and his son were best friends. Then anger flipped the relationship from sweet to sour. Now Saul was filled with suspicion, displeasure, and bitterness toward him. That victory song became a game changer. After this, the relationship with David suddenly became extremely volatile. Subsequently, the evil spirit that was tormenting Saul returned, rather than David's playing calming Saul, it upset him. Suddenly, Saul grabbed a spear and threw it at David attempting to pin him against the wall. This happened twice, but David was able to escape. I do not think Saul wanted to murder David at this point but only to scare and intimidate him.

Before, Saul loved David; now he wanted nothing more than to put fear into his heart. This has happened to all of us. Someone we have a relationship with gets angry and then tries to intimidate us. The "old man" thrives on this anger and intimidation. In 1 John 4:18, the apostle declares, "There is no fear in love; but perfect love casts out fear, because fear has punishment. He who fears is not made perfect in love." If we love someone, we will never attempt to intimate and scare them in our anger! How could we do such a thing to someone we love? Yet, anger knows no reason.

That is why the old man has to be "put off" (Ephesians 4:22). Since King Saul realized David was too well known to simply kill him, he had to devise an alternate plan. Perhaps, he could erase him from the minds and hearts of people by sending him away to the farthest outpost of his army, but this did not deter David. This warrior kept winning and his reputation continued to grow. This only made King Saul fear him even more. Saul knew deep in his heart that God was prospering David in everything he did, and the entire nation loved him. This made David a very real threat to his throne. As his popularity grew, so did Saul's suspicion of him and his motives. Then his anger grew proportionately.

Rather than dealing with his anger, King Saul churned it. So, Saul decided to offer his older daughter Merab to him, if 'he would continue battling the Philistines. He was hoping that David would be killed in battle, and Saul would look innocent. David refused because he felt unworthy to marry a king's daughter, at least this one. Sometime after, King Saul discovered that Michal, his daughter, loved David, and so he offered her to him. His anger had so blinded him that using his daughters as bargaining chips meant nothing to him. We can become so blinded by rage; we don't care who gets hurt.

Rather than pay the usual dowry, Saul wanted David to kill one hundred Philistines. The king thought surely the Philistines will finally kill him. Instead, David took a group of men and fought those Philistines and killed two hundred of these deadly enemies. This only made Saul more afraid and fueled his anger toward David. So, David married his daughter, and Saul obsessed in his anger continually. It was all he cared about. The anger had finally taken over his life. The more David went out to battle, the more victories he won, and the more the people admired him. Now, it became time to get his son and his servants involved in his desire to end David's life. Though Saul knew his son loved David as his closest and dearest friend, he demanded that Jonathon and his servants kill David. Saul knew that they were the only ones who could get close enough to David. Here, anger doesn't concern itself with the feelings of anyone else. Rather than comply, Jonathon hid him.

Jonathon attempted to fully persuade his father Saul to reconsider this terrifying notion. Jonathon reminded his father that David had done nothing but good things for him. He had killed Goliath and brought a great victory to his nation. He had never done anything against his father. He begged his father to rethink the matter and not to be put to an innocent man to death. Suddenly, King Saul repented and vowed to keep David alive. King Saul's son brought David back home, and David's relationship with Jonathon's father was restored.

Since David continued to win victory after victory against the Philistines, this restoration did not last. Reconciliation is based on both of the parties involved continually keeping their flesh, the influence of the Devil, and the world under control. This is not easy. One day, the evil spirit returned and through his influence and torment, a spear came flying through the air once again as David was playing the harp. Most likely, this time it was to assassinate him. David fled that night.

After several other incidences, David fled that night. So, Saul sent messengers to watch David's house, so he could put him to death in the morning. When Michal found out, the daughter of Saul had let him out through a window to escape. She deceived her father's men by making the bed, so it looked like David was still in it. When the messengers came, she told them he was sick. When Saul found out, he ordered them to bring the sick man to him, so he could put him to death. Sometimes anger has no limits. The king was willing to put a sick man to death. He had also forced his daughter to decide between him and her husband. When Saul found out he had been deceived, it only added to his bitterness. As we saw in Psalm 37:8, anger produces only evil upon evil. This wickedness will destroy any relationship in its path. How could it not be this way?

David finally had to even confront Jonathon about their relationship. Now David was concerned whether Jonathon was still on his side. Jonathon did not even know what his father had done, he thought everything was fine. David told him that he could not go back to the palace. Since David was supposed to be regularly at the evening meal with the king, he and Jonathon schemed to lie about David's whereabouts to protect him.

After a couple of evenings without David's presence, Saul confronted his son realizing Jonathon was lying for David and protecting him. In 1 Samuel 20: 30-31, we find out what happens next, "Then Saul's anger burned against Jonathan, and he said to him, 'You son of a perverse rebellious woman, don't I know that you have chosen the son of Jesse to your own shame, and to the shame of your mother's nakedness? For as long as the son of Jesse lives on the Earth, you will not be established, nor will your kingdom. Therefore, now send and bring him to me, for he shall surely die!'"

Now Saul turned the anger he had towards David and directed it to his own son. The King criticized his son and his son's mother. He accused Jonathon of choosing David over him. His son Jonathon did not realize that he was choosing David's future kingdom over the kingdom of their family. He ordered Jonathon to bring David to him so he could murder him. This finally convinced Jonathon his father was determined to kill his best friend. Jonathon now became enraged. Anger and violence often produce more anger and violence in response. Jonathon secretly met with David the next day, and they said their tearful good-byes. Then David departed.

David eventually ended up in the cave of Adullam. He had collected a large group of discontented, debt-ridden, and distressed men to be a part of his ragtag army. This numbered about four hundred. On his journey to the cave, he was helped by a priest named Ahimelech in the city of Nod. David lied to the priest and told him he was on a secret mission for Saul. So, Ahimelech gave him food and offered him the sword of Goliath. Then David departed having lied and put Ahimelech's life on the line.

When Saul was informed, the king went to question the priest. Ahimelech denied knowing anything about Saul's pursuit of David. Rather than doing any investigation, Saul accused the priest of seeking the Lord on David's behalf and murdered him and many in the city. Rage will not reason. Rage does not investigate. Rage does not reason. Rage can lash out in violence. Rage destroys. One of Ahimelech's sons escaped and joined David. While David was on the run, he actually delivered many cities from the hands of the dreaded Philistines. All along this godly man inquired of the Lord with the help of Abiathar the priest and followed God.

While David was on the run from Saul, he wrote several beautiful psalms which were prayers and songs of worship to the Lord God. As Saul kept raging against David, he was worshiping the Lord God. He did not retaliate. Why not? Saul was the Lord God's anointed king. As believers, we are the Lord God's anointed. In 1 Peter 3:7, Peter says, "You husbands, in the same way, live with your wives according to knowledge, giving honor to the woman, as to the weaker vessel, as being also joint heirs of the grace of life; that your prayers may not be hindered." We need to do the same.

While Saul was pursuing David, David spared his life on two occasions. The first occurred in the wilderness of Ziph in the desert of Judah. Saul left his army of 3,000 warriors and went into a cave to relieve himself. He did not realize that David and his men were hiding in it. When the men saw David, they whispered to him that the Lord had put Saul into his hand to slay him. In 1 Samuel 24:6, speaking of David it states, "He said to his men, 'Yahweh forbid that I should do this thing to my lord, Yahweh's anointed, to stretch out my hand against him [Saul], since he is Yahweh's anointed.'" Instead, he cut off a small piece of his robe. When Saul was safely away, David emerged and yelled to Saul. He prostrated himself and addressed Saul as "my Lord the King." David indicated that he had just spared Saul's life, and he had done nothing to deserve death. He did not desire to harm Saul. Saul responded by declaring that David was indeed more righteous than him. David had dealt well with him, but he had dealt wickedly with David.

Saul affirmed that it was obvious that David would be king in place of Him. Then, he begged David to swear that the future king would not destroy his entire family, thus destroying his name on the Earth. David agreed and they both left. All was well until Samuel, the priest, died. Then Saul's temper suddenly flared up. So, he took his daughter Michal, David's wife, and gave her to another man. Once again, his anger knows no bounds and has no dignity. Then Saul began the pursuit of David again to kill him.

The second time, the future king David was hiding on the hill of Hachilah, and Saul came after King Saul. As his army camped on the hill, David had been watching them from another location in the desert. David saw the exact place where King Saul was lying next to Abner, the commander of his army, to protect him. They were in the circle of the camp, and the people were camped around him.

Then David went with Abishai down to the camp, while the people were sleeping. He stood over Saul, while Saul's spear stood upright in the ground close to his head. Abishai whispered that the Lord had delivered Saul into David's hand. In 1 Samuel 26:10-11, it says, "David said, 'As Yahweh lives, Yahweh will strike him; or his day shall come to die; or he shall go down into battle and perish. Yahweh forbid that I should stretch out my hand against Yahweh's anointed; but now please take the spear that is at his head, and the jar of water, and let us go.'" No one heard because a deep sleep from the Lord had overtaken them.

The next morning, David stood up on the adjacent hill and shouted to Abner and his army, "Why have you not protected the king from a sure death by the man who took his spear and jug?" Immediately, Saul recognized David's voice. David again asked Saul why he was worthy of death. He had done nothing wrong and even now had once again not slain Saul, when he had a chance. He would not put his hand against God's anointed.

Saul responded once again with remorse. Saul swore he would not harm David again, since he had spared his life. He recognized how blessed David was by the Lord and would accomplish much and surely prevail against him. They once again departed from each other. This time it was for good. Sometime after this, King Saul and his army were defeated by the Philistines, and he and Jonathon were killed in the fierce battle. The story of Saul's raging anger against David concludes with David eventually becoming King over all the land of Israel.

When Saul became angry at David, he continually fanned the flames of his fiery temper by seeking revenge rather than utilizing the tools we have discovered. David, on the other hand, separated himself, was always gentle, patient, and respectful as he pleaded with Saul to reconsider his bitter actions. When we get angry, we need to separate ourselves, talk ourselves down, release our anger, ask for forgiveness, forgive ourselves, restore relationships, resolve the conflicts, prepare for battle, fear God's discipline, and practice silence.

Workbook Questions

Directions: Now that you have read this chapter, answer the following questions. Answers to the questions regarding the text can be found in chapter nine.

1. According to 1 Samuel 16:18, how did Saul's court officials describe David?

2. Before the slaying of Goliath, what was David's first responsibility that won Saul's affection?

3. After this, what great feat did David accomplish and why was he able to overcome the fear the soldiers could not?

4. After David's victories in battle in which Saul rejoiced, why did he suddenly unleash his temper (1 Samuel 18:8-9)?

5. While David was playing music to soothe Saul, what did Saul do to express his anger on two different occasions?

6. When that did not work, how did Saul attempt to erase David from the minds of the people?

7. Why did Saul choose to offer his oldest daughter to David in marriage? How did this demonstrate the King's continual bitterness toward David and why did David refuse?

8. After this refusal, why did Saul offer his daughter Michal to David?

9. When both plans failed with his daughters, how did Saul want his son to become involved with his angry deeds?

10. What steps should Saul have taken to tame his temper from his jealousy of David?

11. What steps did David attempt or not attempt to prevent Saul's temper from unleashing in response?

12. Have you ever been in any situation comparable to either Saul's unleashed temper or David's righteous response to him? How was it different and how was it the same?

Chapter 7

Fueling the Fire:
A Modern Anecdote

In my counseling practice, I often encounter patients who have inadvertently fueled the flames of their own tempers and gotten themselves into trouble. This was the case of a widowed senior who came to see me. It all started with a barking dog. This dog barked all day and all night. Because my client was retired, he was home much more than most of his neighbors, including the owner of the dog. At first, he tried to ignore it.

Then he put on music to drown out the barking. After this he wore earphones whenever he was home. It wasn't long before he felt he was a captive in his own home. Then he got angry. Anger welled up in him that he had never felt before.

As the days wore on, his anger turned into a deep and dark bitterness for his neighbor and this dog. Why didn't the neighbor do anything? It wasn't long before he was done with it all. He had enough. He tried spraying it with water every time it barked, but the animal seemed to enjoy it. After weeks of this incessant noise, he finally snapped. He began to conceive of a plan to rid himself of this nuisance for good.

He researched numerous poisons that would kill a dog without detection. He wanted a powder that he could insert into a very small piece of food that the dog would quickly consume that had no taste or smell. He justified his behavior by telling himself he was representing all the neighbors, and everyone would be glad the barking had stopped. He would really be a hero in his own neighborhood.

When the dog was dead, maybe the next one will be quiet and docile. Finally, he mixed the poison into the little piece of ground meat and rolled it into a ball. He waited as his heart pounded for the dog to wake up from his slumber. Then he flung it over the fence. As he positioned himself in a different spot in the yard to get it placed just right, he saw something in his peripheral vision. As the ball of poisoned meat lay there, he went to take a look. When the man saw the big, furry stray cat sitting on the fence behind his shed, shivers went up his spine. All along he had been barking at that cat! Who knows how long the cat had been there!

The man suddenly came to his senses. What in the world was he doing? He turned toward the meat and saw that it was still there. He had not climbed a fence in thirty years, but there he was scaling the fence like he was eleven again. Just as he landed on the backyard lawn, the barking dog came running. The animal was so happy to see someone that he hadn't noticed the meat and began jumping up on the man trying desperately to lick his face. The man grabbed the meat and raised his hand into the air.

While the poisoned food was out of reach, he saw the dog differently than he had before. Now the man saw the dog as a pet and not a nuisance and annoyance. He found himself petting the animal. The dog calmed down and wagged his tail. When he arrived home, he contacted animal control, borrowed a cage, caught the cat, and turned the stray over to them. The barking stopped. Then he began to worry. How did he ever get to the place where he would kill someone's dog? I explained to him the power of the flesh.

When it gets angry, it must be dealt with. Left unchecked, Christians are capable of doing heinous things. We began at the start of the dog's barking and looked at where he had gone wrong. He let his anger dictate what he should do, rather than the principles from God's Word. So, what does God's Word say about this situation? As soon as his anger began to come upon him, he should have taken a time-out to search the Scriptures. He needed to determine not only what to do but how to view this difficult situation from the view of His God. The man would have seen that he did not have a problem with the animal; instead, he had a problem with the neighbor. The Lord God's solution for problems in any and all relationships, whether the relationships are close friends or strangers, is to resolve the conflict with His principles. Instead, the man let his anger control him.

Over several sessions, we discussed the critical techniques for extinguishing our fiery tempers rather than putting fuel on them and igniting them further as the senior man had done. We, as Christians, must understand the power of our tempers and how quickly and effortlessly it can take over thoughts, words, and actions.

Workbook Questions

Directions: Now that you have read this chapter, answer the following questions. Answers to the questions regarding the text can be found in chapter nine.

1. Why was the widowed senior so angry with his neighbor?

2. What were some of the ways that the widowed senior attempted to cope with the barking dog?

3. Rather than confront the neighbor, what did the senior decide to do?

4. What caused the senior to come to his senses?

5. What steps should he have taken to tame his temper?

6. What steps did the neighbor attempt or not attempt to prevent the senior's temper from unleashing in response?

7. Have you ever been in a situation where you may have acted like the angry man or the disinterested neighbor?

Chapter 8

Putting Out the Embers: A Special Prayer

When the flames of our fiery tempers have finally been extinguished and only a few embers are still burning, we can use prayer to put them fully out. This chapter is devoted to praying for ourselves and others in regard to how we are handling the taming of our own tempers and responding to the tempers of others. If we need to make changes, prayer is a good starting point. Why? Prayer is a powerful tool in the hands of believers. Our prayers can and will move the hand of our all-powerful God. The Bible is filled with examples of prayer having very powerful effects on the lives of people and nations.

In Genesis 18:22, when Abraham prayed for Lot, his life was spared from the judgment of Sodom and Gomorrah. In Exodus 14:10, when Moses prayed for God's people to be delivered from Egypt, God parted the Red Sea. In Exodus 15:25, when Moses cried out to the Lord God Almighty for the starving Hebrews, God provided manna from heaven. In 1 Kings 17:1, When Elijah, the prophet, prayed for the rain to cease in judgment upon God's people, it did not rain for three- and one-half years. In 1 Kings 18:38, when Elijah asked God to consume his water drenched offering before the 850 prophets of Baal and Asherah, fire came from heaven and burned up his offering while leaving theirs untouched. In Daniel 9:3, when Daniel, the prophet, prayed for Israel's release from Babylonian captivity, God delivered His people through King Cyrus (Ezra 1:1-4). In Luke 1:13, when God's priest Zacharias prayed for his barren wife, she conceived John the Baptist. In Acts 12:5, when the saints prayed for

65

Peter who was guarded by trained soldiers in a prison, he was rescued by an angel.

When King Hezekiah grew deathly ill, he was told by the Prophet Isaiah to get his house in order because the day of his death had come. So, he wept and prayed before God and God answered through a healing and fifteen more years of life (2 Kings 20:1-7). When King Jehoshaphat prayed for victory in battle, God answered that God himself would fight the battle for him and they were to simply stand and watch the deliverance of the Lord. So, the king and his large army marched toward the enemy singing and praising God without swords drawn and the Lord God destroyed their enemies in His great power on the spot (2 Chronicles 20:1-25). These were powerful answers from the Father to the prayers of His people. Even a cursory reading of the Bible produces numerous examples. All of this power is available to believers to control the fire within them.

As we proceed through the temper taming process, we can pray that God would give us or others the conviction, determination, and power to follow these steps through the Holy Spirit. If the taming of our tempers has become habits or practices, then we should pray consistently for change in this important area. Even if we have unleashed our tempers and damaged or even destroyed a relationship, our God can help us reconcile and restore what we have lost. Whether we have struggled with our tempers our whole lives or for a short time, God can work. If we have had a relationship with a believer who has fought this fire, God can change them.

One example is Jonah. When Jonah found himself in the belly of a great fish because he was unwilling to preach to the people of Nineveh, the prophet desperately prayed for deliverance. As a result, God commanded the fish to spew him forth unto the land and Jonah's life was saved from the consequences of his own foolishness (Jonah 2:1-10). God can do the same for our own foolish words and actions when we cannot tame our tempers.

If unbelievers are involved, then we should pray for the conscience within them to do convince them to take the required steps. Then, we should pray for their salvation. Perhaps, God might even provide an opportunity for us to present the gospel and bring them to Christ. When Paul and Silas prayed in the Philippian jail, the Lord God moved in power. Though they were unjustly arrested and watched by a strict jailor, God caused a great Earthquake to occur. As a result, the apostle Paul kept the prisoners from escaping and prevented the Philippian jailor from committing suicide (the jailor would have been killed if the prisoners escaped).

When Paul shared the gospel with him, he and his whole family came to Jesus Christ (Acts 16:25-40). Though this did not involve anger, they were definitely adversaries. If they are uninterested in Him, the Lord may decide to persuade them to control their anger for our sakes. In Egypt, Pharaoh was determined not to allow God's people to go yet God divinely persuaded him to release them by unleashing the plagues of Israel (Exodus 12:31). Though God will not have to bring plagues into the lives of those who cannot control their tempers, the Lord has methods to soften their hearts.

We find a simple prayer pattern in Psalm 5:1-3. He wrote, "Give ear to my words, Yahweh. Consider my meditation. Listen to the voice of my cry, my King and my God; for to you do I pray. Yahweh, in the morning you shall hear my voice. In the morning, I will lay my requests before you, and will watch expectantly." Every morning, he would go before the throne of God with his requests and eagerly watch for God Almighty to work. We will trust in His sovereignty and power to work on our behalf at all times.

Here is a prayer to deal with our anger if it is unleashed?

Dear Heavenly Father,

I have not tamed my temper in many situations; instead, I have allowed my anger to control me, and it has damaged my relationship with (add names). Please help me to follow the principles concerning anger that I have learned in your Word. Give me the willingness and strength through your Holy Spirit to take the necessary time out to prevent any further destruction. I am sorry for what I have done. Please provide the courage I will need to rebuild the relationship with (add names). Then help me to share these principles with (add names) to show them how to deal with me in a holy way when I get angry. I do desire to honor and glorify You in my relationship with (add names).

Here is a prayer if others have unleashed anger upon us:

Dear Heavenly Father,

I have not taken the necessary steps to respond to (add names) uncontrolled temper toward me. (Add names) have allowed their anger to control them, and it has damaged our relationship. Please help me to follow the principles from your word. Give me the willingness and strength through your Holy Spirit to not engage them in their anger so I learn their ways and add even more destruction. I am sorry for what I have done. Please help them to tame their tempers and give me the courage and strength I will need to rebuild the relationship with (add names). Then help me to share these principles with (add names) to show them how to tame their tempers. If they do not know you, please give me an opportunity to share the gospel with them. I do desire to honor and glorify You in my relationship with (add names).

Workbook Questions

Directions: Now that you have read this chapter, answer the following questions. Answers to the questions regarding the text can be found in chapter nine.

1. According to the author, when dealing with prayer concerning the unleashing of our tempers or the tempers of others, what should be our requests to God?

2. What are two examples from the Old Testament of the power of prayer?

3. According to Psalm 5:1-3, what was David's basic method of prayer?

4. Which steps have you had difficulty following in taming your own temper?

5. What steps have you had difficulty following in response to an angry person?

6. Are you presently in a relationship where you have sinned against another due to your anger or responded to others improperly if they have unleashed their tempers?

7. If not, are there relationships from the past that still need restoration due to anger?

8. Based on the truths you have just learned, what will you continue doing in your current relationships and what will you do differently?

9. Based on the truths you have just learned, what will do you need to do with a relationship in the past?

Chapter 9

Answering the Questions: The Author's Key

This chapter is devoted to providing suggested answers to the workbook questions from the text itself. Though the answers might be in the precise or near precise words of the author, it is expected that you will use your own. Some of the questions ask for an analysis of the facts presented and a suggested structure to respond has been provided. Other questions may ask for personal applications of the principles presented. With these, the answers are left up to the readers.

Chapter 1

Understanding the Inferno: A Typical Scenario

1. According to the author, the typical scenario concerned what event?

It's almost family reunion time, and this year I wanted to stay at the big family cabin at the lake.

2. According to the author, what was the conflict about?

For the last three years, everyone else in the family got to pick where we went, and it is my turn now.

Then my younger brother called me and described the horrible time he had last summer at the family cabin with his asthma. Apparently, the altitude is too high and the air too thin for him. He spent the entire week trying to catch his breath. Now he wants to have the reunion near a beach, where he can breathe freely. That is not what I want! So, we got into this big argument.

3. When the author compares the expression of our anger in relationships with the building of a wall, the spreading of a fire, and the spitting of venom, what does he mean?

Anger is able to build a wall so high that any words or actions to restore the relationship can't be heard or seen. It can spread like fire to anyone connected to the relationship. Their families, friends, church members, co-workers, and fellow students may be forced to take sides and divisions can occur that may never be restored. The ones who will remain neutral may be ostracized by either or both of the parties. Like a dangerous snake, an uncontrolled temper can spit its wicked venom poisoning every relationship in its path.

4. According to 1 Corinthians 1:10-12 and 12:25, what should never be found in Christian relationships?

In 1 Corinthians 1:10, Paul entreats the Corinthians to be unified and resolve their disputes...Later in chapter 12, verse 25, he explains, "That there should be no division in the body, but that the members should have the same care for one another." This is critical principle for believers to follow in their relationships.

5. According to 1 Thessalonians 5:13 and Hebrews 12:14, what are we to seek in our relationships?

We are told throughout the Scriptures that the Lord God wants peace and unity. In 1 Thessalonians 5:13, Paul writes, "Be at peace among yourselves." Then in Hebrews 12:14, it says, "Follow after peace with all men." Anger destroys this peace and unity in our relationships.

6. According to Psalm 37:8, what might the unleashing of our temper actually add to a relationship?

Often times, anger will actually add to the conflicts we are trying to resolve. In Psalm 37:8, the wise King David warns that unleashing our temper "leads only to evildoing."

7. Have you had a similar experience?

Here, you might desire to write something personal that could be shared if used in a group study.

Chapter 2

Extinguishing the Blaze: A Scriptural Principle

1. According to John 2:17, why can we not use the example of Jesus cleansing the temple to justify righteous anger?

In John 2:17, after Jesus cleansed the temple, the apostle recorded, "His disciples remembered that it was written, 'Zeal for your house will eat me up.'" The Greek word which is translated "zeal" means "intense feeling, passion, and very strong emotion." It does not mean, nor does it imply anger. This is a direct quote from Psalm 69:9 and the Hebrew word is also translated "zeal," not anger. This word speaks of the passionate devotion and fervor which Jesus possessed.

2. According to the author, why did Jesus cleanse the temple, but the apostles did not?

The Lord Jesus had so much "fervency in spirit" and "passion" for preserving the purity, holiness, and integrity of God's temple that He was compelled to clear out the money changers on two different occasions. This was done from His authority as the Son of God which is why the apostles never did this.

3. According to Mark 3:5, what actually made Jesus angry and sad in the one incident recorded?

The passage reads thus, "When he had looked around at them with anger, being grieved at the hardening of their hearts, he said to the man, 'Stretch out your hand.' He stretched it out, and his hand was restored as healthy as the other.'" As this powerful miracle occurred, several Jewish leaders were watching. They taught that there was to be no working [labor] on the Sabbath. In their minds, "healing" someone was basically working; therefore, there was to be no healing.

4. According to the author, what are two reasons we should not "fight an argument out?"

Though some people may suggest that it is a wonderful idea to "fight something out," this does not work and is never God's way; therefore, it is definitely not something we should become engaged in.

5. According to the author, what is the Scriptural principle in his words?

The key truth that should guide us in the taming of our tempers is "we must put away all anger in our relationships."

6. How would you express the principle in your own words?

Here, you might desire to write something personal that could be shared if used in a group study.

7. How would you rewrite this principle to make it even more personal to your life (using your name and situation)?

Here, you might desire to write something personal that could be shared if used in a group study.

8. Why do you think this principle might be important in your life right now?

Here, you might desire to write something personal that could be shared if used in a group study.

9. How would you rate yourself on the percentage of times you followed the Scriptural principle in the past when you were annoyed?

Here, you might desire to write something personal that could be shared if used in a group study.

Directions: Put a horizontal mark and your name where you are on the percentage line.

| 0% | 25% | 50% | 75% | 100% |

Chapter 3

Controlling the Heat:
A Biblical Explanation

1. According to Jesus, what commandment is broken when we express our anger (with Bible verses)?

In Matthew 5:21-24, Jesus condemned anger as murder of the heart as He addressed the true heart intent of the sixth commandment. When our tempers issue forth into angry thoughts, words, or any actions (short of murder), these are also sins of "murder" but "murder of the heart."

2. According to Jesus, how is the expression of our anger a kind of "murder?"

In Matthew 5:21-24, Jesus condemned anger as murder of the heart as He addressed the true heart intent of the sixth commandment. When our tempers issue forth into angry thoughts, words, or any actions (short of murder), these are also sins of "murder" but "murder of the heart."

3. According to Matthew 5:21-24, what expressions of anger are actual sins?

According to the Lord, a person cannot be angry with his brother (in thoughts), and then say, "Raca" or "You fool" (in words). Also, murder (in actions) is implied. Since our words are less violent than actions and are sins, then harmful actions from a murderous heart are also sins.

4. According to Ephesians 4:32 and Colossians 3:8, what are Christians supposed to do with their angry feelings?

Paul continues to elucidate God's truth concerning anger. He teaches this principle clearly from two different passages. In Ephesians 4:31, the apostle commands, "Let all bitterness, wrath, anger, outcry, and slander, be put away from you, with all malice."

In Colossians 3:8, he then repeats, "But now you also put them all away: anger, wrath, malice, slander, and shameful speaking out of your mouth." Paul uses two different words in his similar commands. We are to remove our anger. The word translated "wrath" refers to a quick-tempered rage and "anger" is more the general idea. Both are condemned. We should remove them.

5. According to Psalm 37:8, what is the eventual result of all expressions of anger?

This is taught in the Old Testament as well. In Psalm 37:8, King David urges his readers, "Cease from anger, and forsake wrath. Don't fret." Here he utilizes the three Hebrew terms which designate general anger, quick tempered wrath, and even hot rage respectively. Then the inspired writer commands us to cease, forsake and don't act on them. Why? As we saw, "It leads only to evildoing."

6. According to Ephesians 4:26, what aspect of our anger is not a sin?

Something from outside the person is prompting the inward feeling. The angry feelings are on the inside, but someone or something is provoking or stirring it up.... It comes upon a person without their volition....Paul recognizes the fact that Christians may become angry without premeditation, and the feelings may come upon them suddenly. The feelings of anger are not the sin; it is what they do with the angry feelings that are the sin.

7. According to Paul's use of the term "anger," what would be three qualities of this anger which is not sinful?

This verb "be angry" is in the present passive imperative tense. It conveys three crucial meanings. First, the verb "be angry" is in the "imperative," which means it is a command.

Second, it is present tense. This denotes continuous action in present time. This means that the anger does not just arise and leave as fast as it came, it could stay awhile, or it could come back.

8. According to the author, what is the first way that feelings can actually be sinful (provide the Bible verses)?

The first can occur when we dwell on the incident and allow our anger...tempers to grow. The Bible calls this process "churning our anger." In Proverbs 30:33, King Solomon absolutely advised against this action, "For as the churning of milk produces butter, and the wringing of the nose produces blood; so, the forcing of wrath produces strife." We can churn what happened within our hearts like one makes [churns] butter by continuously thinking angry thoughts about the person.... We can spend nights planning revenge against the person turning our angry feelings into a raging fire. In Hosea 7:6, the prophet describes evil men in these words, "For they have prepared their heart like an oven, while they lie in wait plotting. Their anger smolders all night, in the morning it burns like a flaming fire" (DEJ).

9. According to the author, what is the second way that feelings can actually be sinful (provide the Bible verses)?

The second way in which feelings can become sinful is to become angry so often that we develop the habit of anger. This anger comes from within us not from without as Paul is discussing. Sometimes, we become angry because we have developed a habit of angry outbursts. We...allowed our temper to be unleashed so often that it becomes our "go to" response whenever things do go our way or people disagree with us.

10. According to the author, what is the third way that feelings can actually be sinful (provide the Bible verses)?

The third is the enjoyment of getting angry and letting our tempers flare. This also comes from within and not without. In Galatians 5:24...These outbursts of anger can be enjoyed as an expression of our passion and lust. We can lust after the moments where we can experience the full passion of our raging anger.

11. According to Galatians 5:22-23, what fruit of the Spirit should we express rather than anger?

Christians are to remove the feelings of anger and instead replace them with patience and self- control.

12. In what ways have these truths impacted your life and relationships?

You might write something personal that could be shared in a group study.

Chapter 4

Stomping Out the Fire: A Godly Technique

1. According to Proverbs 6:27; 29:28, what analogy could be used to think of our feelings of anger?

In this chapter, we will discuss godly techniques to help us stomp the fire of our tempers out. I am using the analogy of fire because it is easy to think of our anger as a ball of fire in our inner hearts. When Solomon speaks of the problem of pursuing after lust, he uses the analogy of fire. In Proverbs 6:27, Solomon asked, "Can a man scoop fire into his bosom, and his clothes not be scorched?" (DEJ)....in Proverbs 29:8, Solomon utilizes the fire analogy for the devastation that one's anger can bring. It sets a city on fire. He explains, "Mockers set a city on fire, but wise men turn away anger" (DEJ)... As we have seen in Galatians 5:20, "outbursts of anger" proceed from the lusts of the flesh. So, let us think of our feelings of anger as a ball of fire that may well up in us and could be thrown at others through our angry thoughts pouring forth in harsh words and evil deeds.

2. According to the author, what does it actually mean to "put away" or "put off" anger?

We can immediately throw that ball of fire at the people who have transgressed us and destroy the relationships we have with them. Or we can extinguish the fire God's way. The Lord's method of dealing with anger is to "put it away" or "put it off." These were mentioned briefly; now, let's take a closer look at both. In Ephesians 4:31, he uses the first term and in Colossians 3:8, Paul utilizes the second term. Both describe this process. The Greek word which is translated "put it away" means to remove it or take it away.... The Greek word for "put it off" refers to putting off an article of clothing or putting something aside. We should put away or take off the anger that we might be feeling. In our analogy, we need to take action to stomp out the fire that has been created.

3. According to Psalm 4:4, what is the first step in dealing with our ball of fire? Why?

First, we are to go to our bed. Though this might sound strange with careful consideration, it makes perfect sense. They lived in a Bedouin world of tents.

Like our bedrooms of today, the room with the "bed" would be separate from the other rooms by a covering. This would be the only place someone could be alone. He does not mean to literally go to our beds but to remove ourselves from the situation which is provoking the anger.

We might call it today taking a "time out." We leave the situation provoking our rage and the people who we are about to explode upon, if at all possible.

4. According to Psalm 4:4, what is the second step and what shall you be doing?

Second, Christians should "meditate." Biblical meditation is nothing like what is seen in the world. The Hebrew word "meditate" literally means "to speak or talk." It carries the idea of talking things over with ourselves and God. We mull things over... and add God's input from His Word. So, we are talking the whole situation over with God through prayer and the Word. We are attempting to tame out tempers by acknowledging...God does not want our anger expressed. This will not glorify Him and will only destroy relationships in the process.

5. According to Psalm 4:4, what is the third step and why is this important?

While we are involved in this process, David explains the next step, "Be still." Stop everything else. All of our thoughts, words, and actions come to a halt. Our body stops. We stop and take the necessary time to process the situation in our minds. This important word also carries the sense of relaxing and releasing something. He is [basically] saying, "Calm down and let it go." This Hebrew word translated "be still" can also mean "be silent, still, wait." In Psalm 37:8, the psalmist helps us with this concept when he says, "Cease from anger and forsake wrath. Don't fret, it leads to evildoing." The word "cease" is a very powerful Hebrew word. The word means to "drop and relax." We drop the matter, let the issue go, and completely relax in our decision to follow God.

6. According to Luke 17:3-4, what is the fourth step we should take to reconcile the relationship after unleashing our temper?

In Luke 17:3-4, Jesus states, "Be careful. If your brother sins against you, rebuke him. If he repents, forgive him. If he sins against you seven times in the day, and seven times returns, saying, 'I repent,' you shall forgive him."

In this passage, Jesus presupposes that someone will repent. The "repenting" implies that the other asks for forgiveness. When we have unleashed our anger upon others, we intuitively know that we ought to repent and ask for forgiveness because we are convicted by our consciences (Romans 2:15).

7. According to the author, what is step five and what does the Bible say about our sins?

The next step we should take is to forgive ourselves for our angry outburst. Though obvious, this is often difficult. We must forgive ourselves for our sin as God has forgiven us. If we do not, we will feel defeated, broken, and unable to build the relationship anew. We do not have to carry this burden; instead, we can be free of it once and for all. The best method in doing this is to review how God has forgiven our sins.

In Colossians 2:13-14, Paul explains how God has nailed our sins and their resultant judgment which he calls "debts" to the cross of Jesus Christ, "You were dead through your trespasses and the uncircumcision of your flesh. He made you alive together with him, having forgiven us all our trespasses, wiping out the handwriting in ordinances which was against us; and he has taken it out of the way, nailing it to the cross." We must tell ourselves that Christ shed His blood to take its judgment on our behalf.

8. According to Galatians 6:1, what does it mean to restore a relationship and how does one do this (Revelation 2:5)?

In Galatians 6:1, Paul explains this important concept when he exhorts the many saints in the city, "Brothers, even if a man is caught in some fault, you who are spiritual must restore such a one in a spirit of gentleness." Here, Paul is speaking of someone who is caught in a sin and the other believers help restore them. If the sin is only against God, they repent and accept His forgiveness. If others have been sinned against, then they must do the same with them.

Untamed tempers destroy relationships, and they need to be restored. The Greek word which is translated "restore" can mean "to render fit, sound, or complete; to mend or repair what has been broken; to equip and prepare someone for something; to complete." In this context, it means to mend or repair what was broken.... When a relationship has been broken, it must always be mended. All the holes must be patched and repaired so the relationship is whole again. How does this happen? What do we actually do to mend the relationship? It is through the utilization of many loving words and actions. These words and actions rebuild relationships in the same way as they were used to build them in the first place.

9. According to Ephesians 4:26, what must be done before the sun sets? If this cannot be accomplished what does the author suggest?

In Ephesians 4:26, Paul states, "'Be angry, and don't sin.' Don't let the sun go down on your wrath." The word "wrath" is a different word than Paul used in the first part of the verse. Here, the apostle is focusing on the instigation of the anger. Paul stipulates that it should be done before the sun goes down. We should not go to bed angry. If we cannot deal with it at the moment, we should set a time or make an appointment for a full discussion to resolve it when those involved are calm.

10. According to Proverbs 10:12 and 1 Peter 4:8, how should we handle the smaller transgressions and briefly how would we do it?

The first principle in resolving conflicts is to cover over the less important issues in love. In Proverbs 10:12 it says, "Hatred stirs up strife, but love covers all wrongs." The parallel passage is found in 1 Peter 4:8, "And above all things be earnest in your love among yourselves, for love covers a multitude of sins." Both Solomon and Peter wrote of the importance of covering over many sins in love....

Our love should cover over the small annoyances, minor irritations, and often, even the greater transgressions that might occur as we interact in our various relationships with people. The word translated "cover" means to "cover over, conceal, or hide." When we love others, we should...conceal the smaller problems between us and others by letting them go and not even mentioning them at all.

11. According to the author, how should we handle most of the larger transgressions and briefly how would we do it?

This brings us to the second principle which is to decide together on the larger issues in unity. The biblical decision-making process has several critical steps which I will only mention.

12. According to Ephesians 4:27 and Romans 7:23 who must we battle and how do we win (the eighth step)?

All of these processes will prevent an opportunity for the Devil to destroy our relationships. In Ephesians 4:27, Paul concludes his thought with these words, "And do not give place to the Devil." The word translated "give" means "to reach out the hand to furnish." The word translated "place" means "a portion or space marked off for a specific purpose, or an occasion for acting on something." An untamed temper reaches out our hands to the Devil to provide him with a specially marked off spot in our relationships to destroy them.... As I mentioned earlier, we have a serious enemy within which resides in our bodies. In Romans 7:23, Paul describes his battle with the flesh, "But I see a different law in my members [flesh], warring against the law of my mind, and bringing me into captivity [battle] under the law of sin which is in my members."

13. According to Acts 12:11, if we cannot win the battle, who will intervene and how (ninth step)?

Next, we must fear God's discipline. In Hebrews 12, the author explains God's discipline process. As a loving father disciplines and trains his children so does God. This refers to God using trials as a tool to help us stop sinning. In verse 11, the author writes, "All chastening seems for the present to be not joyous but grievous; yet afterward it yields the peaceful fruit of righteousness to those who have been exercised thereby."

14. According to the author we should practice silence (tenth step) regularly. In James 3:2-6, what are three analogies used to describe the tongue and how do we control it?

Now, there is a critical action that must be taken to allow ourselves the time to handle this ball of fire. It is "silence." We [as believers] need to restrain our mouths! We need to keep our tongues under control, so the situation can be dealt with properly...James describes the power of an uncontrolled tongue and the fury it can unleash. In chapter 3 of James, the brother of Jesus utilizes three analogies to express the power of our words: a wild horse, an out-of-control ship, and a raging forest fire.... Here, James explains that we must tame the tongue as we tame a horse. Then he adds this comment, "Behold, the ships also, though they are so big and are driven by fierce winds, are yet guided by a very small rudder, wherever the pilot desires." James speaks of piloting the tongue to control it.... Now, he asserts that the flames of tongue must be put out.

15. What principles in this chapter were you unfamiliar with, struggled with, and were able to implement in your life?

Here, you might desire to write something personal that could be shared if used in a group study.

Chapter 5

Preventing the Burn: A Holy Response

1. According to the author, what is step one?

First, we respond by asking for a time out. We can leave the angry person to allow them to follow the principles we just discussed. This may mean that we have to literally walk away. Rather than the angry person suggesting a time out, we can. Sometimes, people cannot control themselves and our walking away will defuse the situation immediately.

2. According to Proverbs 22:24-25, what may happen if we continually engaged in another's anger toward us?

In Proverbs 22:24-25, Solomon warns us, "Do not associate with a hot-tempered man; or go with one who harbors anger, you might learn his ways and find a snare for yourself (DEJ)."

Yet, if at all possible, we should stop associating with them when they are raging. This will lessen the chance that we will learn their ways by raging ourselves in response or falling into their snare and trap by engaging in the same actions.

3. According to Proverbs 15:1 and Proverbs 25:18, in what way should we answer the angry person if we cannot leave (step two)?

Second, we should respond with a gentle answer. If we must engage in a discussion of the situation, we ought to respond gently. In Proverbs 15:1, Solomon pens, "A gentle answer turns away wrath, but a harsh word stirs up anger." Then, in Proverbs 25:15, he continues with this adage, "By patience a ruler is persuaded. A soft [gentle] tongue breaks the bone." This wise man explains in the first passage how a gentle response can turn away someone's wrath. It will take "make them retreat" with their fireball of anger aimed at you. Why? In the second passage, Solomon provides one answer: the soft response breaks their bones. It will cause them to feel terribly guilty for their raging because there is such a dramatic contrast between your response and their reaction. Since Proverbs contain general principles of living, these are not hard and fast rules.

4. According to Proverbs 15:18, in what critical way should we answer the angry person if we cannot leave (step three)?

Third, we should also provide a patient answer. This is a "patience" that calms.

5. According to Romans 12:17, what is step four and why is it important?

Fourth, we ought always to show respect while speaking. If we respond, it should be done in honor. Though someone may be angry at us, the showing of respect will keep us from engaging in the same behavior.

6. According to the author's discussion of step five, is our forgiveness of someone who unleashed their anger on us dependent upon their repentance and why?

This forgiveness process is not dependent on others asking for... forgiveness first, making restitution, or even accepting...consequences. In the following passages, our forgiveness is not contingent upon these...actions by the transgressor.... True believers simply forgive as God has forgiven them. In the following passages, Jesus does not add conditions to his commands to forgive.

7. According to the Lord Jesus, who should be forgiven and who should not if they transgressed us? (Provide verses)

All must be forgiven because Jesus uses the inclusive terms, "debtors," "anyone," and "everyone."

8. What principles in this chapter were you unfamiliar with, struggled with, and were able to implement in your life?

Here, you might desire to write something personal that could be shared if used in a group study.

9. Are there other principles from the Scriptures which you think should be included?

Here, you might desire to write something personal that could be shared if used in a group study.

Chapter 6

Fanning the Flame: An Ancient Portrait

1. According to 1 Samuel 16:18, how did Saul's court officials describe David?

In 1 Samuel 16:18, they described David in these critical words, "Then one of the young men answered, and said, 'Behold, I have seen a son of Jesse the Bethlehemite who is skillful in playing, a mighty man of valor, a man of war, prudent in speech, and a handsome person; and Yahweh is with him.'"

2. Before the slaying of Goliath, what was David's first responsibility that won Saul's affection?

So, young David was called to play music to soothe Saul's pain, whenever he was tormented. At first, Saul loved David and made him his personal armor bearer...when Saul went out to battle, he depended on David to carry additional weapons and to protect him if needed.

3. After this, what great feat did David accomplish and why was he able to overcome the fear the soldiers could not?

Since the Lord God had delivered him on so numerous occasions from lions and bears, he would face and defeat this arrogant warrior. With a slingshot and five smooth stones, young David killed this mighty giant of a man. It was over quickly in God's power.

4. After David's many victories in battle in which Saul rejoiced, why did he suddenly unleash his temper (1 Samuel 18:8-9)?

After each of these victories, the young women would stand outside with their tambourines and other musical instruments to celebrate the victory. Now they sang, "[King] Saul has slain...thousands, and David his ten thousands." Saul became...jealous, and his anger was aroused. In 1 Samuel 18:8-9, it is described this way, "Saul was very angry, and this saying displeased him. He said, 'They have ascribed to David ten thousands...to me they have ascribed only thousands.

What can he have more but the kingdom?' King Saul watched David from that day forward."

5. While David was playing music to soothe Saul, what did Saul do to express his anger on two different occasions?

Subsequently, the evil spirit that was tormenting [King] Saul returned, rather than David's playing [the harp] calming Saul, it upset him. Suddenly, Saul grabbed a spear and threw it at David attempting to pin him against the wall. This happened twice, but David was able to escape. I do not think Saul wanted to murder David at this point but only to scare and intimidate him.

6. When that did not work, how did Saul attempt to erase David from the minds of the people?

Since King Saul realized David was too well known to simply kill him, he had to devise an alternate plan. Perhaps, he could erase him from the minds and hearts of people by sending him away to the farthest outpost of his army, but this did not deter David. This warrior kept winning and his reputation continued to grow.

7. Why did Saul choose to offer his oldest daughter to David in marriage? How did this demonstrate his continued bitterness toward David and why did David refuse?

So, Saul decided to offer his older daughter Merab to him, if 'he would continue battling the Philistines. He was hoping that David would be killed in battle, and Saul would look innocent. David refused because he felt unworthy to marry a king's daughter, at least this one.

8. After this refusal, why did Saul offer his daughter Michal to David?

Sometime after...Saul discovered that Michal, his daughter, loved David, and so he offered her to him. His anger had so blinded him that using his daughters as bargaining chips meant nothing to him. We can become so blinded by rage; we do not care who gets hurt in the process.

Rather than pay the usual dowry, [King] Saul wanted David to kill one hundred Philistines. The king thought surely the Philistines will finally kill him. Instead, David took a group of men and fought those Philistines and killed two hundred of these deadly enemies. This only made Saul more afraid and fueled his anger toward David. So, David married his daughter and Saul obsessed in his anger continually.

9. When both plans failed with his daughters, how did Saul want his son to become involved with his angry deeds?

Now, it became time to get his son and his servants involved in his desire to end David's life. Though Saul knew his son loved David as his closest and dearest friend, he demanded that Jonathon and his servants kill David. Saul knew that they were the only ones who could get close enough to David. Here, anger doesn't concern itself with the feelings of anyone else. Rather than comply, Jonathon hid him.

10. What steps should Saul have taken to tame his temper from his jealousy of David?

The answers can be found in comparing King Saul's behavior with the following steps. He should have separated himself, talked himself down, released his anger, asked for forgiveness, forgave himself, restored their relationship, resolved their conflict, prepared for battle, feared His discipline, and practiced silence.

11. What steps did David attempt or not attempt to prevent Saul's temper from unleashing in response?

The answers can be found in comparing future King David's behavior with the following steps. He could have suggested an amount of time to separate, but Saul was King, so he ran. He always provides a gentle response, maintained the required respect, and fully forgave the person.

12. Have you ever been in any situation comparable to either Saul's unleashed temper or David's righteous response? How was it different and how was it the same?

Here, you might desire to write something personal that could be shared if used in a group study.

Chapter 7

Fueling the Fire:
A Modern Anecdote

1. Why was the widowed senior so angry with his neighbor?

This was the case of a widowed senior who came to see me. It all started with a barking dog. This dog barked all day and all night. Because my client was retired, he was home much more than most of his neighbors, including the owner of the dog. At first, he tried to ignore it.

2. What were some of the ways the widowed senior attempted to cope with the barking dog?

At first, he tried to ignore it.

Then he put on music to drown out the barking.

After this he wore earphones whenever he was home. It wasn't long before he felt he was a captive in his own home.

Then he got angry. Anger welled up in him that he had never felt before.

As the days wore on, his anger turned into a deep and dark bitterness for his neighbor and this dog. Why didn't the neighbor do anything?

It wasn't long before he was done with it all. He had enough. He tried spraying it with water every time it barked, but the animal seemed to enjoy it.

3. Rather than confront the neighbor, what did the senior do?

After weeks of this incessant noise, he finally snapped. He began to conceive of a plan to rid himself of this nuisance for good.

He researched numerous poisons that would kill a dog without detection. He wanted a powder that he could insert into a very small piece of food that the dog would quickly consume that had no taste or smell. He justified his behavior by telling himself he was representing all the neighbors, and everyone would be glad the barking had stopped. He would…be a hero in his own neighborhood.

When the dog was dead, maybe the next one will be quiet and docile. Finally, he mixed the poison into the little piece of ground meat and rolled it into a ball. He waited as his heart pounded for the dog to wake up from his slumber. Then he flung it over the fence. As he positioned himself in a different spot in the yard to get it placed just right, he saw something in his peripheral vision

4. What caused the senior to come to his senses?

As the ball of poisoned meat lay there, he went to take a look. When the man saw the big, furry stray cat sitting on the fence behind his shed, shivers went up his spine. All along he had been barking at that cat! Who knows how long the cat had been there!

5. According to the techniques for taming of our tempers, what steps should the senior have taken to tame his temper?

The answers can be found in comparing the senior's behavior with the following steps: separate yourself, talk yourself down, release your anger, ask for the other's forgiveness, forgive yourself, restore the relationship, resolve the conflict, prepare for battle, fear his discipline, and practice silence regularly.

6. According to the author's discussion on responding to an angry person, what steps did the neighbor attempt or not attempt to prevent the senior's temper from unleashing in response?

The answers can be found in comparing the neighbor's behavior with the following steps: suggest a time of real separation, provide a very gentle response, maintain the required respect, and fully forgive the person.

7. Have you ever been in a situation where you may have acted like the angry man or the disinterested neighbor?

Here, you might desire to write something personal that could be shared if used in a group study.

Chapter 8

Putting Out the Embers: A Special Prayer

1. According to the author, when dealing with prayer concerning the unleashing of our tempers or the tempers of others, what should be our requests to God?

As we proceed through the temper taming process, we can pray that God would give us or others the conviction, determination, and power to follow these steps through the Holy Spirit. If the taming of our tempers has become habits or practices, then we should pray consistently for change in this important area.

Even if we have unleashed our tempers and damaged or even destroyed a relationship, our God can help us reconcile and restore what we have lost. Whether we have struggled with our tempers our whole lives or for a short time, God can work.... If unbelievers are involved then we [as believers] should pray for the conscience within them to do convince them to take the required steps. Then, we should pray for their salvation. Perhaps, [our] God might even provide an opportunity for us to present the gospel and bring them to Christ....If they are uninterested in Him, the Lord may decide to persuade them to control their anger for our sakes.

2. What are two examples from the Old Testament of the power of prayer?

In Genesis 18:22, when Abraham prayed for Lot, his life was spared from the judgment of Sodom and Gomorrah.

In Exodus 14:10, when Moses prayed for God's people to be delivered from Egypt, God parted the Red Sea.

In Exodus 15:25, when Moses cried...to the Lord God Almighty for the starving Hebrews, God provided manna from heaven.

In 1 Kings 17:1, when Elijah...prayed for the rain to cease in judgment upon God's people, it did not rain for three-and-one-half years.... In 1 Kings 18:38, when Elijah asked God to consume his water drenched offering before the 850 prophets of Baal and Asherah, fire came from heaven and burned up his offering while leaving theirs untouched.

In Daniel 9:3, when Daniel (prophet) prayed for Israel's release from captivity, God delivered His people through King Cyrus (Ezra 1:1-4).

In Luke 1:13, when God's priest Zacharias prayed for his barren wife, she conceived John the Baptist.

In Acts 12:5, when the saints prayed for Peter who was guarded by trained soldiers in a prison, he was rescued by an angel.

When King Hezekiah grew deathly ill, he was told by the Prophet Isaiah to get his house in order, because the day of his death had come. So he wept and prayed before God and God answered through a healing and fifteen more years of life (2 Kings 20:1-7).... When King Jehoshaphat prayed for victory in battle, God answered that God himself would fight the battle for him and they were to simply stand and watch the deliverance of the Lord. So, the king and his large army marched toward the enemy singing and praising God without swords drawn and God destroyed in His great power delivered their enemies to them on the spot (2 Chronicles 20:1-25).

3. According to Psalm 5:1-3, what was David's basic method of prayer?

We find a simple prayer pattern in Psalm 5:1-3. He [David] wrote, "Give ear to my words, Yahweh. Consider my meditation. Listen to the voice of my cry, my King and my God; for to you do I pray. Yahweh, in the morning you shall hear my voice. In the morning, I will lay my requests before you [God] and will watch expectantly." Every morning, he [David] would go before the throne of God with his requests and eagerly watch for God Almighty to work. We will trust in His sovereignty and power to work on our behalf at all times.

4. Which steps have you had difficulty following in taming your own temper?

Here, you might desire to write something personal that could be shared if used in a group study.

5. What steps have you had difficulty following in response to an angry person?

Here, you might desire to write something personal that could be shared if used in a group study.

6. Are you presently in a relationship where you have sinned against another due to your anger or responded to others improperly if they have unleashed their tempers?

Here, you might desire to write something personal that could be shared if used in a group study.

7. If not, are there relationships from the past that still need restoration due to anger? 8. Based on the truths you have just learned, what will you continue doing in your current relationships and what will you do differently?

Here, you might desire to write something personal that could be shared if used in a group study.

8. Based on the truths you have just learned, what will you continue doing in your current relationships and what will you do differently?

Here, you might desire to write something personal that could be shared if used in a group study.

9. Based on the truths you have just learned, what will do you need to do with a relationship in the past?

For questions 4-9, you might desire to write something personal that could be shared if used in a group study.

Conclusion

Finding the Eternal Solution: The Only Way

As we conclude this book, I would like to leave us with some final thoughts about our God. We have a God of forgiveness who was willing to sacrifice His Son on the cross for us. If you read this entire book and realized that you do not understand salvation or have never received Christ as Lord and Savior, then I would like to provide that life-changing opportunity. Please do not skip this section; it may be the most important in your life.

From all outward appearances, humans seem "good" and attempt to live decent lives. This is man's concept of himself. This is not God's concept. The Almighty's view is that people all over the world and throughout the ages sin, sin, and sin again (Romans 3:23). This is a terrible and utterly destructive condition. Yet, they have ramifications that are far worse. These sins condemn us to everlasting divine retribution.

Though described briefly in the Old Testament, the Lord Jesus Christ clearly announced and proclaimed the future punishment to come. Contrary to popular belief, Jesus did not only speak of love, grace, and mercy, He also spoke of the coming judgment for sin. He declared that the judgment of sin would be everlasting punishment in a place He called "Hell." The Lord portrayed this place as an eternal inferno (Matthew 18:8) where there would be the weeping (from the sorrow) and gnashing of teeth (from the agony and anguish of suffering) continually into eternity (Matthew 8:12; 13:42, 50; 22:13; 24:51; 25:30; Luke 13:28). This is a terrifying fate for all who mankind who die without salvation in Christ.

Why must people face this horrific punishment? Though God is a God of love, grace, and mercy, He is also a God of great holiness, righteousness, and justice (Psalm 89:14,18). These attributes are just as much a part of His divine nature as His love, grace, and mercy. You have broken God's law as we all have, and the penalty must be paid. This began with the first man Adam (Genesis 3:1-7). When this occurred, His love, grace, and mercy surfaced, and a provision was made. Someone else would have to take man's place and pay the penalty. Someone who had never transgressed Him, who would never deserve punishment, and would fulfill all of God's Laws, would be substituted in man's place. This was the Son of God, Jesus Christ.

As the God-Man, He would pay the penalty for our sins in His death on the cross. Once done, the Lord God made only one provision for people to appropriate what His Son had done on the cross for them. This provision is receiving Jesus Christ as Savior and Lord. Though I cannot possibly share with you this good news in the confines of this book, I would love for you to consider purchasing my book entitled, *Finding the Light: The Kingdom of Heaven and How To Enter It*. It can be found for sale on Amazon.com. It is inexpensive and contains the full gospel message for your consideration. This message is so important and extensive that it cannot adequately be contained in a few pages at the end of a book.

If you are a believer, you must go out into the world and put away your anger. These principles are to be lived and shared with others. You now have the tools to tame your temper and make your relationships last a lifetime. Go live them out and share them with others!

ABOUT THE AUTHOR

Dr. Donald Jones is currently a Christian Pastoral Counselor with thirty-eight years of experience in the fields of pastoral ministry, public education, and Christian counseling. He carries degrees and certificates from four major universities and from a variety of educational institutions. He has been a professor of Languages and Bible, a television commentator, and a featured speaker at a variety of events and seminars at churches, schools, and other organizations across the United States. He is a member in good standing of several secular and Christian professional organizations. Dr. Jones has been a published author since 1976. For further information view his website at www.donjonesphd.com.

www.ingramcontent.com/pod-product-compliance
Lightning Source LLC
Chambersburg PA
CBHW031602040426
42452CB00006B/387